Praise for [illegible]

"Sandy Forsythe's words often [illegible] God is working on in my life, and I frequently send her a response saying, 'How did you know?' The Lord speaks to Sandy in such special and profound ways, and her intimacy, transparency, and vulnerability in her relationship with Him pour out in her devotions. Her notes and takeaways are a front-row seat to her daily conversations with Jesus. I highly recommend *Jesus Confidential*."
— Laura Simmons
Atlanta, Georgia, and Los Angeles, California

"When I'm having a bad day, sometimes I just want to know that someone is on my side. By sharing Scripture and truths combined with personal stories and beautiful photos, Sandy Forsythe's devotional *Jesus Confidential* has helped me appreciate that I have more than just someone: I have God! He is here for me, He understands my heart, and He will reassure me."
— Bonnie Rowsey
Dallas, Texas

"I was very blessed to receive *Jesus Confidential* during a time in my life when I was suffering from a tremendous loss. The Scriptures and encouragement each day helped me to heal and know that God will never fail me—He will carry me through my suffering with His unfailing love and grace."
— Shelly Peown
Hilton, New York

"Sandy Forsythe's gift of spiritual communication is clearly God-given."
— Bill Anderson, Lori Anderson's husband (to whom this devotional is dedicated)
Dallas, Texas

"Sandy Forsythe's daily devotional keeps me grounded. On good days, the readings remind me to slow down, appreciate all of my blessings, and make room for God in my life. On dark days, they remind me that He is always with me: If I have faith in Him, I will be fine. Sandy's messages refresh my soul. The pictures she includes remind me that God shows His presence in so many ways—I just need to take the time each day to see it and give Him thanks. Drinking my morning coffee while reading *Jesus Confidential* has become a ritual that I look forward to every day."
— Lyn Magee
Allen, Texas

"In an exhausting and constantly changing world, we need reminders of truth. Of permanence. Of purpose. We all need help at some point in our lives to 'fix our eyes not on what is seen, but on what is unseen, since what is seen is temporary, but what is unseen is eternal' (2 Corinthians 4:18). If you are weary and worn, here is a resource for your soul. Sandy Forsythe's *Jesus Confidential* offers sips of living water for our thirsty souls. Reminders of what matters. Of what is eternal. Let these devotions help you wrestle your attention off of the seen, the immediate, the temporary, and place it instead on the life-changing truth of the Bible. Nothing else will satisfy. We need these reminders!"
— Lynelle Zandstra
Dallas, Texas

"I've known Sandy for decades. She has a gentle soul and is a modern-day tender warrior. When I'm around her, her 'cup runs over,' and the life of Jesus simply spills out of her. I'd encourage you to let *Jesus Confidential* help shepherd your soul like it has mine."
— Kevin East
President and CEO, Mentoring Alliance
Tyler & Waco, Texas

"I love reading Sandy's devotional every morning. She has such a unique way of consolidating multiple truths from God's precious Word into just a few brief comments. Her devotions are encouraging and often convicting; they will challenge you to search your heart and soul."
— Deb Fredette
Cohasset, Massachusetts

"In a world that is saturated with bad news, Sandy Forsythe's daily devotional has been instrumental in creating an opportunity for me to refocus, recenter, and realign myself to God's Word every day. As a busy mom of three kids, I am grateful for *Jesus Confidential*'s nudge to make time for Him to minister to me as His child. It's a spiritual hug that speaks straight to my heart."
— Landon Tillery
Dallas, Texas

"Sandy has a beautiful gift of communicating God's words of love and grace while simultaneously challenging her readers to press in and allow the Spirit to transform their hearts. Her writings always leave me feeling inspired, deeply loved by the Savior, and challenged to let the Spirit do His holy work in me."
— Carolyn Atkinson
The Church at Agape Outpost
Breckenridge, Colorado

"We have such busy lives, but *Jesus Confidential*'s short daily devotions are such a wonderful way to focus on what is important in life. They are written by a real person: a regular, over-scheduled mom who has a passion for offering love and encouragement to others. Sandy Forsythe summarizes her own devotional readings and reflections in a concise and meaningful way, and she even shoots the beautiful photos that are included—which help me remember the takeaway for the day!"
— Renee Kapinus
Madison, Wisconsin

“As a mom of a son who serves in the United States Marine Corps, the daily devotions in *Jesus Confidential* have kept my thoughts from going places they are not meant to go. I am so grateful for Sandy’s obedience to God as she listens to Him, and for her willingness to share His love and promises.”
— Jeanie Bishop
Norwell, Massachusetts

“Starting my day with the uplifting spiritual message of *Jesus Confidential* is a positive reminder that every day is a blessing from God. Reading Sandy Forsythe’s words helps me to have communication with the Holy Spirit and fills me with the confidence of knowing that God is with me wherever I go.”
— Kathleen Gaffney
New York, New York

“Sandy Forsythe’s inspirational messages are extremely timely and applicable. Her words are a gift from God, reminding me to have faith as I apply them to my own life, and the intentional and artistic images that accompany each message always put a smile on my face. In our high-pressure and fast-paced lives, where we often feel that we have little time to do what is demanded of us, *Jesus Confidential* is a refreshing break.”
— Dawn Herring
Rancho Santa Fe, Colorado

“Sandy Forsythe is devout, steadfast, and unwavering in her devotion to Jesus. *Jesus Confidential* will inspire you to dig deeper and stay longer in the things of God. You will watch with amazement as she cuts through the fog of our daily existence and captures the prize for the high upward call of God in Christ Jesus.”
—Joe Martin, Jr.
Senior Pastor, C3 Trinity Church, Dallas

Jesus Confidential

A daily devotional meeting with God

Sandy Forsythe

Dear Veronica!
May God Bless you
richly as you seek His face!
♡ Sandy
Feb. 2023

Printing and binding in South Korea through Bolton Associates, Inc., Grass Valley, California.

Cover design: Jessica Johnson
Cover image: Photo by Sandy Forsythe
Interior design: Jessica Johnson

ISBN: 978-1-7324362-1-3 paperback
ISBN: 978-1-7324362-3-7 ebook

All proceeds from this book will go to support the work of Share God With Us, Inc.

Our ministry shares God's Word by donating Scripture cards to both individuals and organizations across the USA, Europe, Africa, and Russia. We also collect stories of God's intervention in today's world and post them online to share the hope he gives us as we encourage others in his love.

To learn more, or to order Scripture cards, go to www.ShareGodWithUs.com.

www.ShareGodWithUs.com

Dedicated to my beloved friends
Lori Anderson, 1954–2020,
and Susan Neibel, 1958-2020

Foreword

I first met Sandy Forsythe in a women's Bible study that I led in a Dallas church. I immediately noticed her eager eyes. It's so easy to tell when someone is hungry for the Word of God. I remember wondering who this woman was—with her evident passion for the things of God, and her insightful comments. I assumed she was a seasoned Bible teacher who was visiting one of the church's small groups.

I was surprised to find out later that she wasn't a teacher—just a humble disciple. I was surprised again when I read Sandy's first book, *Three Messages From God*, and observed the spiritual maturity therein. Later she introduced me to her daily devotional messages, which came from a disciplined morning regimen of reading Scripture and classic Christian devotionals such as *Streams in the Desert* and *My Utmost for His Highest*. Then in quiet contemplation, she would wait for the Lord to point to a personal "takeaway."

What you hold in your hands is 365 days of these morning conversations with God.

You will quickly discover that Sandy is not a dispenser of inspirational fluff. While she writes with deep conviction about God's love and goodness, she also talks about the tough stuff: sin, obedience, suffering. Her messages have spiritual substance, moral heft. I could tell I was hearing from the heart of someone who follows Jesus Christ for real.

We need the voices of wise disciples like Sandy. As I write this, we are coming out of a pandemic and are in the midst of global turbulence. I find myself longing for something pure, for words of eternal wisdom and truth, coming from the mouths of "ordinary people" who've walked a lifelong path of obedience to Christ. I believe you will find words such as these in *Jesus Confidential*, and I pray that they will help you keep your eyes fixed on Christ.

Julie Lyons

Author of *Holy Roller:Finding Redemption and the Holy Ghost in a Forgotten Texas Church* (WaterBrook Press, 2009)

Introduction

What you hold in your hands are my private moments with God: *Jesus Confidential*. They are notes, Scriptures, and takeaways distilled from my daily quiet times with the Lord. I began sharing them with my two closest friends as they battled cancer, hoping to encourage them and nourish our friendships during a time when many miles separated us.

Lori was my anchor whenever I needed to talk; she shared her life and wisdom with me. She was one of the most generous, kind listeners I have known.

Susan taught me how real God is and how to pray. One time I asked Susan if we could be prayer partners. Sure, she said. But it was like a novice runner trying to keep stride with an Olympic legend! She did what we all hope friends will do for us, taking time to come to my aid right at the moment I needed help, and I did the same for her.

While my friends lived in Dallas, I lived in Boston. It bothered me that I couldn't pop over to their homes and cheer them up, or bring flowers or soup or fold laundry. I was at a loss for how to help when the distance was so great. It took me a while to realize that the only thing I could do was be with them in spirit. So, I began to give them the gift I had in my hands. I shared these same notes from my time with the Lord each day.

While Susan and Lori were fighting for their lives, I took a bit of a health detour as well. I am fortunate, however, that my medical issue was non-life-threatening. My friends gave me a wonderful perspective: The Giant Cell tumor that ate into my femur created a mechanical problem and hurt like heck, but it wasn't going to kill me. I feel blessed to have my leg, even with a lot of metal in it.

I learned the hard way, however, that it is extremely difficult to spend quality quiet time with the Lord when you are in physical pain. It is hard to be yourself when you don't feel like yourself. So to redirect myself from my pain and help my friends grapple with their own, I decided to share my personal quiet time notes with Lori and Susan. The text messages they sent back were rich; they gave me more than I gave them, I am sure.

Over the last few years, the sharing of these quiet time notes has grown organically to many other friends. I discovered that of lot of us need a boost to help us through a dry spot. Now, I send out the Quiet Time Notes and Takeaway as a text message, and I post them on Facebook, Instagram, and my website, www.ShareGodWithUs.com. Sending it out is like giving the people I know a hug each morning. I love it!

As you read this devotional, please know I am not a theologian. I am just a mom who asks God each morning what He wants me to take away from our time together. I'm blessed to have a stack of devotionals that I read, written by true writers who are wise and on fire for the Lord. I also read blogs written by brilliant men and women who post each morning. And of course, I start with my Bible. Before I read anything, I ask God to be with me, to show me what He wants me to learn for this day. If I forget to do this, it's like digging in quicksand!

I find it amazing that the God of all creation will sit with me for a few hours and help me learn about Him. I am blessed to be like a colander letting His message pass through me to my friends.

What you hold is a few years' worth of my morning quiet times—edited to save you from some of my quicksand days! What I do is a fairly simple process. First, I ask God to help me discern what He wants me to learn that day. Depending on what time my dog wakes me up, I read anywhere from five to ten devotionals and online blogs, taking note of the main point in each. Next, I re-read all my notes and I highlight what seems most important. Then, I distill the notes once again, beginning to type the text message I will send out that day. I always re-read it several times to see if it feels right. Finally, I ask God for the one takeaway that He wants me to have—the one thought for me to hold onto that day.

I don't rush things. I never have preconceived notions of what the takeaway will be, and it is always a surprise. Once I have it, I look through my photos for an image to cement the message in my brain. I am very visual, and the picture helps me remember what He shared with me that day.

Most of the pictures come from everyday life. These past few years my husband Carl and I have lived in Cohasset, Massachusetts; Dallas, Texas; and Breckenridge, Colorado, so most of the pictures are taken around these communities. You will notice that most are of natural things; I would suggest that one of the most important ways God reveals Himself is through nature. It is just so beautiful that I can't resist, so I snap a lot of pictures of creation.

You'll recognize Brinkley, our ever-expressive, 90-pound English Lab, in quite a few photos. He is a big lug of a dog—sometimes super-smart, other times taking a minute to connect the dots. He is six years old and sheds way too much fur, but he makes us laugh. When Lori died, Brinkley knew my heart was broken and stayed by my side as I wrote her eulogy. He loved me even more when Susan died, expressing much-needed love.

I hope these devotions are a blessing to you. I hope you read them when the birds are chirping at the crack of dawn. I hope they lift you over a tough spot so you're not alone. As I shared with my good friends, I share God's goodness with you. I know He will meet you just as He met Lori, Susan, and me.

May He bless you with His favor,

Sandy

"Call to Me, and I will answer you, and show you great and mighty things, which you do not know."

—Jeremiah 33:3 NKJV

January 1

QUIET TIME NOTES:

- God started his best work in darkness—then He brought healing light.
- "Do not be overcome by evil, but overcome evil with good." —Romans 12:21
- The problem is that we look to our past and repeat it instead of allowing God to create the new life He has for us.
- "Darkness was over the surface of the deep…And God said, 'Let there be light,' and there was light." —Genesis 1:2-3
- "Set your minds on things above, not on earthly things." —Colossians 3:2

My Takeaway:

God's best work began in darkness.

January 2

QUIET TIME NOTES:

- Who can ever count how much we lose through self-indulgence?
- According to Genesis 11:31, Terah (Abraham's dad) set out from Ur to go to Canaan but ended up settling in Haran.
- I wonder if God passed His blessing—and His promise—on to Abraham because Terah stopped short of Canaan. Do we stop short too?
- "Rather, clothe yourselves with the Lord Jesus Christ, and do not think about how to gratify the desires of the flesh." —Romans 13:14
- We miss blessings when we live selfishly.

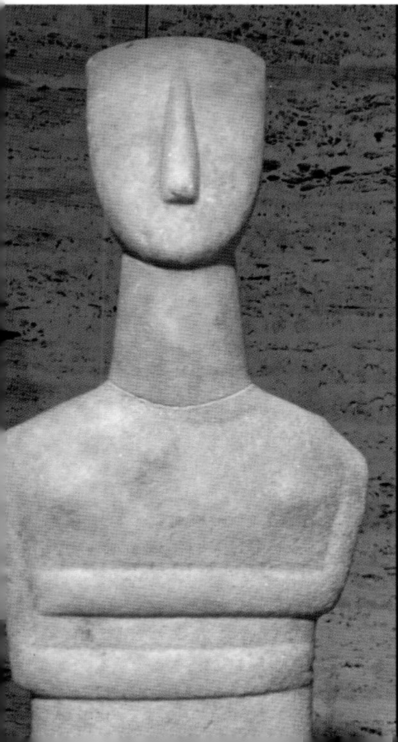

My Takeaway:

We miss blessings when we live selfishly.

January 3

QUIET TIME NOTES:

- Only those who enter God's promise are protected.
- For more than 100 years, people watched the ark being built. But because of their unbelief, they weren't allowed to enter it and live. If you hear God's voice, listen.
- "Today, if only you would hear his voice, do not harden your hearts..." —Psalm 95:7-8

My Takeaway:

I had many notes today, but this one is jumping off the page: "Listen up—God wants to save you. Get in His boat while you still can."

January 4

QUIET TIME NOTES:

- We choose fear or faith.

- Our greatest need is not happiness; it's forgiveness.

- "The beginning of anxiety is the end of faith, and the beginning of true faith is the end of anxiety." —George Mueller, from *Streams in the Desert*

- Pray until your heart believes God—then begin thanking Him for the answer.

- "If you believe, you will receive whatever you ask for in prayer." —Matthew 21:22

My Takeaway:

We choose faith or fear.

January 5

QUIET TIME NOTES:

- Peace comes from a profound faith decision.
- May I surrender to the Lord through every trial and find peace despite life's continual changes.
- "You will keep in perfect peace those whose minds are steadfast, because they trust in you." —Isaiah 26:3
- Paul made a profound faith decision to live in Christ and have Christ live in him (John 15:1-9, Galatians 5:22-23).
- "For it is God who works in you to will and to act in order to fulfill his good purpose." —Philippians 2:13

My Takeaway:

Faith that brings peace comes from a decision to trust God.

January 6

QUIET TIME NOTES:

- My actions reveal my attitude toward God.
- Pay attention to your motives; character matters.
- "You have made for yourself other gods…and turned your back on me." —1 Kings 14:9
- "I heard the voice of the Lord saying, 'Whom shall I send?'" (Isaiah 6:8). A persecuted Christian asked, "Are you willing to answer this prayer?"
- "Serve wholeheartedly, as if you were serving the Lord, not people." —Ephesians 6:7
- We usually only see a small corner of God's masterpiece.

My Takeaway:

My actions reveal my attitude toward the Almighty.

January 7

QUIET TIME NOTES:

- The clamor of our idols robs us of peace.
- "Rest in Me before I get crowded out and your troubles take over." —A.J. Russell, *God Calling*
- "Enter his gates with thanksgiving and his courts with praise..." —Psalm 100:4
- "The idols of the nations are silver and gold, made by human hands...Those who make them will be like them." —Psalm 135:15, 18

My Takeaway:

Be still my soul, so I can hear God over my noisy idols.

January 8

QUIET TIME NOTES:

- It takes trials to grow faith.
- Trust God to sort out your jumbled, confused thoughts.
- You never learn faith in the comfort zone.
- We have to be immersed in the floodwaters in order to truly stand on God's promises.
- "When you pass through the waters, they will not sweep over you." —Isaiah 43:2

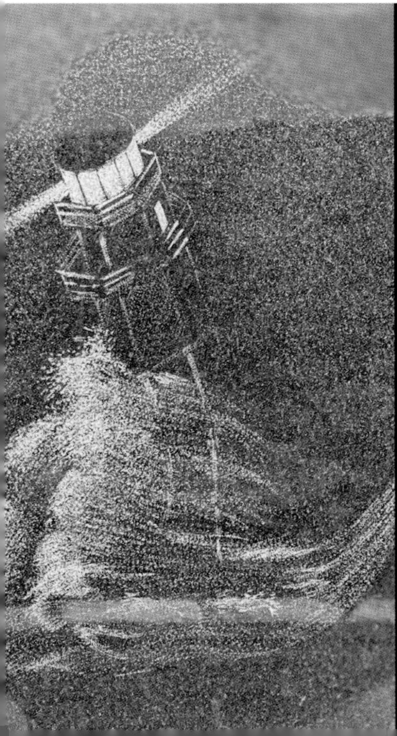

My Takeaway:

It takes trials to grow faith.

January 9

QUIET TIME NOTES:

- Struggles birth strength.
- "Those who know your name will put their trust in you." —Psalm 9:10
- I long to forget the world and pursue God without distractions.
- "To be known and not fully loved is our greatest fear." —Tim Keller
- God's delays provide the necessary preparation. "When he heard that Lazarus was sick, he stayed where he was two more days." —John 11:6
- When Lazarus was raised from the dead, people saw Jesus' power!

My Takeaway:

Struggles birth real strength, and God's patience is a blessing.

January 10

QUIET TIME NOTES:

- I can't be a witness if I censor myself.

- I quit social media thinking I'd live by my convictions, and then I stopped sharing my daily devotions! God sat me down and reminded me of the one Scripture that started my sharing years ago:

  "You are my witnesses," declares the LORD, "and my servant whom I have chosen, so you may know and believe me and understand that I am he." —Isaiah 43:10

- I can't be God's witness if I quit.

My Takeaway:

Neither servants nor soldiers choose where they work, and I can't be God's witness if I quit.

January 11

QUIET TIME NOTES:

- May fear of losing faith be my biggest fear.
- "Fear is unreasoning, unjustified terror which paralyzes needed efforts to advance." —Franklin D. Roosevelt
- "Do not fear, for I have redeemed you; I have summoned you by name; you are mine." —Isaiah 43:1
- Problems distract us from devotion to Christ.
- If you expose yourself to something repeatedly, it changes your brain.
- Do not be misled: Bad company corrupts good character. Come back to your senses! —1 Corinthians 15:33-34, paraphrased

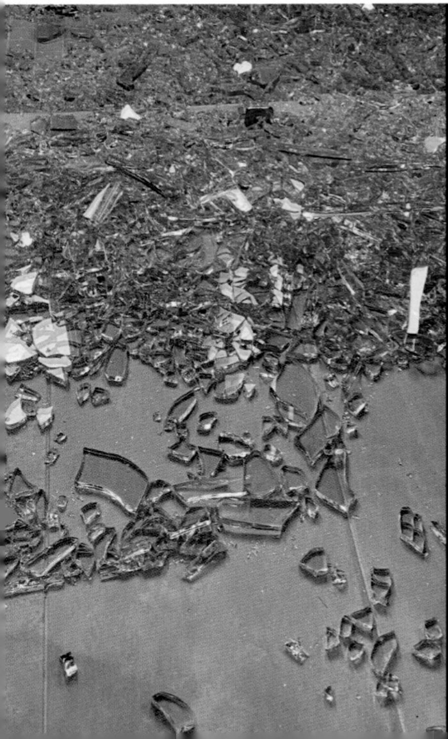

My Takeaway:

May fear of losing faith be my biggest fear.

January 12

QUIET TIME NOTES:

- We can feed our fears or pursue peace.
- Fear breeds more fear and has an insane ability to exaggerate.
- God hedges us in for our protection, but often we see the wrong side of the hedge and misunderstand Him.
- "Those who plow evil and those who sow trouble reap it. At the breath of God they perish." —Job 4:8-9
- If there is a kindness or any good thing I can do, do it now and don't delay—I may never pass this way again. —Stephen Grellet, paraphrased
- Use all God gives you to help others, including your time.

My Takeaway:

We have one chance to use our time but two options: feeding fear or pursuing peace.

January 13

QUIET TIME NOTES:

- Facing our fears builds endurance that leads to freedom.
- It is hardship that builds character, not the easy life.
- You will only reach your destiny if you do what you fear.
- “The worst danger we face is the danger of being paralyzed by fear.” —Harry Truman
- “As soon as their feet touch the water...the river will stand up like a wall.” —Joshua 3:13 NLT
- FEAR = False Evidence Appearing Real

My Takeaway:

Facing our fears builds endurance that leads to freedom.

January 14

QUIET TIME NOTES:

- God knows our inner thoughts and still has compassion.
- "Be kind and compassionate to one another, forgiving each other, just as in Christ God forgave you." —Ephesians 4:32
- "What is man that you are mindful of him?" —Psalm 8:4 NKJV
- As I write this, my dog is having an active dream. God knows what it is, but I'll never know; it's a secret between them! God's thoughts are above our thoughts (Isaiah 55:9).

My Takeaway:

God knows our inner thoughts and still came to forgive us. He is outrageously kind and compassionate!

January 15

QUIET TIME NOTES:

- Devastating events are not eternal, but choosing God's power is.
- Disastrous events often produce critical change.
- Don't let fear sabotage your potential: "What I feared has come upon me; what I dreaded has happened to me." —Job 3:25
- "A godly life is lived one decision at a time." —Elizabeth George
- We must learn to thrive in a continually changing world. We have access to God's power, and He never changes. Use His power or lose it!
- May our choices reflect an eternal perspective.

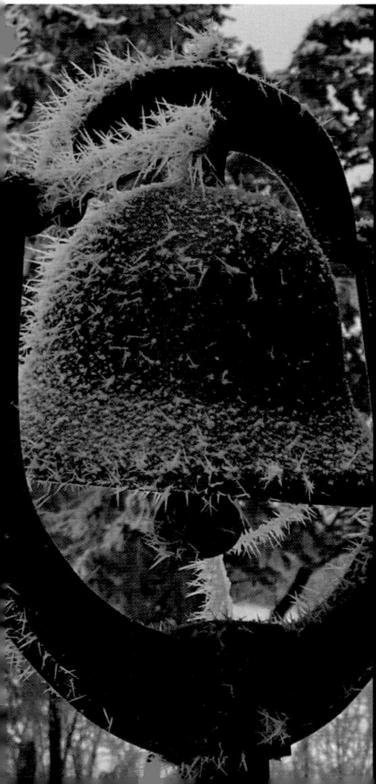

My Takeaway:

Devastating events are not eternal, but choosing God's power is.

January 16

QUIET TIME NOTES:

- Believe God will help you, and you'll get out of the pit.

- "Our doubts are traitors, and make us lose
  what we might oft win, by fearing to attempt."
  —William Shakespeare, *Measure for Measure*

- God equips us for service as we go through the storms of life.

- "They spread a net for my feet—
  I was bowed down in distress.
  They dug a pit in my path—
  but they have fallen into it themselves."
  —Psalm 57:6

- "When you consciously choose to practice operating in a mindset of gratitude...you will get a surge of rewarding neurotransmitters."
  —Dr. Carolyn Leaf, *Switch on Your Brain Every Day*†

† Dr. Carolyn Leaf, *Switch on Your Brain Every Day*, 2018, Baker Publishing Group.

My Takeaway:

Believe God will help you, and you'll get out of the pit.

January 17

QUIET TIME NOTES:

- Cooperate with God to scrub compromised faith out of your life.
- Don't waste another day to grow in God's grace.
- Deepening trust in God's goodness erases worry.
- Be watchful for Satan's offer of compromise.
- "Lean not on your own understanding..." —Proverbs 3:5

My Takeaway:

Cooperate but don't compromise.

January 18

QUIET TIME NOTES:

- True faith preserves and perseveres.
- "If I cannot do great things, I can do small things in a great way." —Martin Luther King Jr.
- Jesus is either your Lord or He is not.
- "The midwives, however, feared God and did not do what the king of Egypt had told them to do…" —Exodus 1:17
- "[Faith] is the envelope in which every request to Me should be placed." —A.J. Russell, *God Calling*
- "There is no other god who can rescue like this!" —Daniel 3:29 NLT

My Takeaway:

True faith, small as it may be, carries us through defeats.

January 19

QUIET TIME NOTES:

- God first and foremost, others second, self last.
- The more we focus on ourselves the more miserable we become.
- We each have a God-given responsibility to make an eternal impact.
- "For God is not a God of disorder but of peace." —1 Corinthians 14:33
- "But Moses again pleaded, 'Lord, please! Send anyone else.' Then the Lord became angry with Moses." —Exodus 4:13-14 NLT

My Takeaway:

My order of priority: God first and foremost, others second, self last.

January 20

QUIET TIME NOTES:

- Accepting God's love eradicates self-rejection.
- "Though you have made me see troubles...you will restore my life again." —Psalm 71:20
- Living in fear of rejection will eventually cause the very rejection you fear.
- You demonstrate how people should value you by the way you value yourself.
- God has already given you His full acceptance.
- "You are precious to me. You are honored, and I love you." —Isaiah 43:4 NLT
- "Come to me...and I will give you rest." —Matthew 11:28

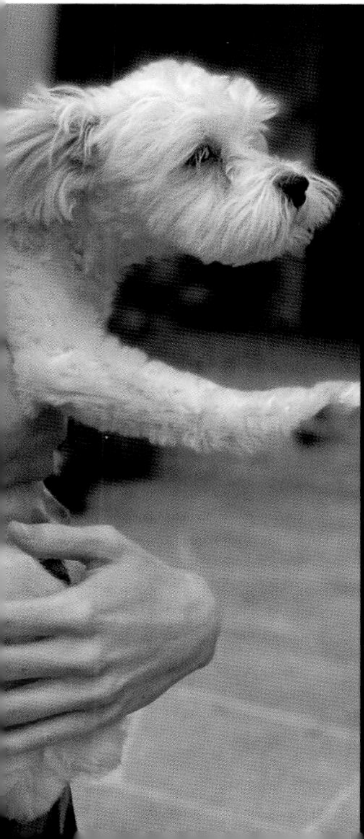

My Takeaway:

Facing the truth that God loves you will change the way you love yourself. Accepting God's love eradicates self-rejection.

January 21

QUIET TIME NOTES:

- You'd never choose sorrow, but it is sorrow that teaches deep-seated faith.
- "Now choose life, so that you and your children may live." —Deuteronomy 30:19
- All of our sorrows and difficulties are opportunities to think deeply, learn, and exercise faith.
- "God will meet you where you are and take you to where He wants you to go." —Dr. Tony Evans
- "Though he slay me, yet I will trust in Him." —Job 13:15 KJV

My Takeaway:

Choosing to trust God in the day of sorrow impacts my family's future.

January 22

QUIET TIME NOTES:

- Stillness is part of following our Savior.
- "There is no music during a musical rest, but the rest is part of the making of the music." —*Streams in the Desert*
- "God did not lead them along the main road that runs through Philistine territory, even though that was the shortest route to the Promised Land." —Exodus 13:17 NLT
- "The people of Israel looked up and panicked when they saw the Egyptians overtaking them…But Moses told the people…'The Lord himself will fight for you. Just stay calm.'" —Exodus 14:10b, 13a & 14
- In a world of haste, we will stay on the righteous path if we walk with God.

My Takeaway:

Stillness is part of following our Savior.

January 23

QUIET TIME NOTES:

- Christ assures us that our troubles are tunnels for today, not forever.
- "God…calls us in the middle of all the unexplained absurdities of life." —Henri Nouwen, *You Are the Beloved*
- "God is our refuge and strength, an ever-present help in trouble." —Psalm 46:1
- When we feel like we are going through the darkest tunnel, God is just as close as when we walk under the brightest skies.
- "My prayer is not that you take them out of the world but that you protect them from the evil one." —John 17:15
- "It is well, even when it's not." —Sylvia Gunter

My Takeaway:

Christ assures us that our troubles are tunnels for today, not forever.

January 24

QUIET TIME NOTES:

- When we devote ourselves to serving others, there is less time to obsess about ourselves.
- "Aaron and Hur held his hands up…" —Exodus 17:12
- "The work is too heavy for you; you cannot handle it alone." —Exodus 18:18
- Nearly half of full-time ministers eventually resign because of the stress it causes their families.
- "But the dove found no resting place for the sole of her foot, and she returned into the ark to him…" —Genesis 8:9 NKJV
- "Hanging back and refusing to serve is a form of thievery—it robs the Church." —Dr. Charles Stanley

My Takeaway:

You are refreshed by giving others rest.

January 25

QUIET TIME NOTES:

- God wants us to make it home, so he gave us the House rules.
- The 10 Commandments, paraphrased from Exodus 20:

1. Keep God first in everything!
2. Worship God alone.
3. Revere His name.
4. Rest once a week.
5. Love and respect your parents.
6. Keep life sacred.
7. Keep your love life pure.
8. Earn what's yours.
9. Tell the truth always.
10. Be grateful for what you have.

My Takeaway:

God wants us to make it home, so he gave us the House rules.

January 26

QUIET TIME NOTES:

- Christ cleans us with His love every day if we stay in His life-giving water.
- Nibbling on a verse here and there won't renew and clean our mind. We need to soak in God's Word—just like a dirty skillet needs to soak in hot water in order to get all the junk removed.
- "Throw off…your former way of life…Instead, let the Spirit renew your thoughts and attitudes."
  —Ephesians 4:22-23 NLT
- We must let go of yesterday if we want to fulfill God's will today.
- I chose you and appointed you—now go and love each other. —John 15:16-17, my paraphrase

My Takeaway:

Christ cleans us with His love every day if we stay in His life-giving water.

January 27

QUIET TIME NOTES:

- If my love for God has reservations, I relinquish His promises.
- Our restless haste makes us reckless.
- We must entrust ourselves completely and unreservedly to the Lord, as a husband and wife commit themselves to each other at the marriage altar.
- “He has given us his very great and precious promises, so that through them you may participate in the divine nature…” —2 Peter 1:4

My Takeaway:

If my love for God is reckless or offered with reservations, I relinquish His promises.

January 28

QUIET TIME NOTES:

- God sends His loving assurance that He is with us.
- "Do not be afraid, for I am with you." —Isaiah 43:5
- "All the days ordained for me were written in your book before one of them came to be." —Psalm 139:16
- "My peace I give you…Do not let your hearts be troubled and do not be afraid." —John 14:27
- "Go forward fearlessly…Be very sure that when you come to it the waters will part and you will pass over to your promised land of freedom." —A.J. Russell, *God Calling*

My Takeaway:

Today's note is for my friend Susan, who is very close to going home. Yet God sends His loving assurance that He is with us.

January 29

QUIET TIME NOTES:

- Our expectations of control distract us from God.
- "Indeed…He will surely come out to me, wave his hand over the place and heal the leprosy." —2 Kings 5:12
- Elisha didn't do what Naaman had expected, and Naaman became furious because his expectations were not met.
- Pay attention to how you react to distractions. Are your eyes on the distractions or Christ?
- Don't think because your sins are "small" they have escaped the notice of God.

My Takeaway:

Our expectations cause us to react like we're in control. We are not, but God is. Our desire to control is rooted in sin.

January 30

QUIET TIME NOTES:

- Don't procrastinate—prioritize eternity.
- My doubts do not negate God's promises.
- Every moment, I can choose the eternal over the temporary.
- People are more important to God than projects.
- "The longer man makes plans to do something, the less chance there is that he'll ever do it." —Irina Ratushinskaya
- "Jesus replied, 'What is impossible with man is possible with God.'" —Luke 18:27

My Takeaway:

Don't procrastinate—prioritize eternity. An eternal perspective will cause you to act.

January 31

QUIET TIME NOTES:

- The fruit of the Spirit is a sumptuous feast for hungry souls.
- We don't want to be exposed as frauds on Judgment Day. Let's be salt and light in this world while we're still living in it.
- "We are 'salt' and 'light,' both of which influence their environment in far greater proportion than their size or amount." —Dr. Jim Denison
- "We must meet the uncertainties of this world with the certainty of the world to come." —A.W. Tozer

My Takeaway:

A small bit of salt changes everything.

February 1

QUIET TIME NOTES:

- Our hearts reveal terror or trust.
- In Heaven, "There is joy without sorrow, comfort without suffering, love without inconstancy, rest without weariness."
—Arthur G. Bennett, *The Valley of Vision*
- "For this is my doing." —1 Kings 12:24
- The remedy for weariness and the prescription for rest is acknowledging that "This is my doing."
- "Since you are precious and honored in my sight, and because I love you…"
—Isaiah 43:4 (Let this sink in—God loves you!)
- My treatment of others is the measure of my affection toward God.

My Takeaway:

Our hearts reveal terror or trust.

February 2

QUIET TIME NOTES:

- God will help us if we ask. He is waiting for us.
- "Don't be afraid," the prophet answered, "Those who are with us are more than those who are with them." —2 Kings 6:16
- "Concerning the work of my hands, command ye me." —Isaiah 45:11 KJV
- Have I ever realized what it means to be able to summon at will the God of the world?
- "But to My subjects I have given the right to enter My Presence when they will." —A.J. Russell, *God Calling*
- "The angel of the LORD encamps around those who fear him, and he delivers them." —Psalm 34:7, cited in a devotional by a persecuted Christian

My Takeaway:

God wants us to ask for His help.
He is ready and waiting.

February 3

QUIET TIME NOTES:

- God's business vs. self-business.
- "But they made light of it and went their ways, one to his own farm, another to his own business." —Matthew 22:5 NKJV
- "Render…to God the things that are God's." —Mark 12:17
- "Jesus replied, 'You must love the Lord your God with all your heart, all your soul, and all your mind.' [And]…'Love your neighbor as yourself.'" —Matthew 22:37-39 NLT

My Takeaway:

Who does my life serve the most: God or self?

February 4

QUIET TIME NOTES:

- We rise on God's winds.
- Don't be shocked when battles follow blessings.
- Planes always take off into the wind, because it is the wind that lifts their wings. The suffering we endure is God's wind. We need suffering to soar!
- "But those who hope in the LORD will renew their strength. They will soar on wings like eagles…" —Isaiah 40:31
- GRACE = God's Riches At Christ's Expense
- You can't see the wind, nor can you always see the hand of God. But that doesn't mean God isn't working on your behalf.

My Takeaway:

We can't see the wind that causes us to rise.

February 5

QUIET TIME NOTES:

- Unexpected grace outweighs unexpected grief.
- "I passed through the Red Sea by a way I did not expect." —Arthur G. Bennett, *The Valley of Vision*
- It takes a Red Sea to experience the most profound grace. In our toughest moments, God's grace is sweetest.
- "The LORD gives strength to his people; the LORD blesses his people with peace." —Psalm 29:11
- The Christ who is in me is so much greater than what He does for me. He is my reward!
- You can't explain grace during grief—you can only experience it.

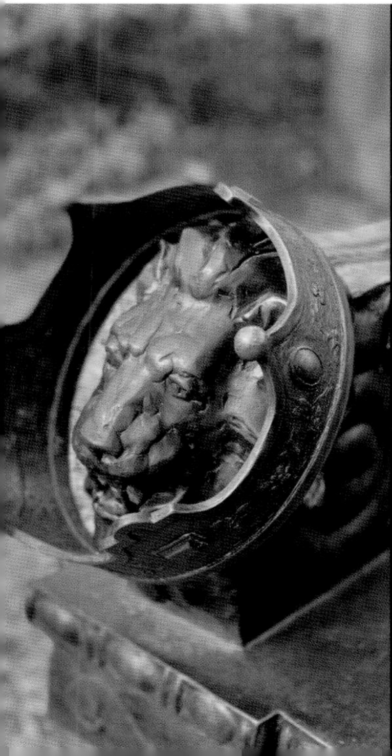

My Takeaway:

God's grace is greater than grief.

February 6

QUIET TIME NOTES:

- Following God's guidance in the small things changes the big things.
- The Spirit warns us in the stillness of our heart, but we often ignore Him to our hurt.
- "Show me the way I should go, for to you I entrust my life." —Psalm 143:8
- Those around us are attracted or repelled by the little things we do.
- When we follow the crowd, we are no danger to the Devil. (From a persecuted Christian.)
- "Becoming envious, [they] took some of the evil men from the marketplace, and gathering a mob, set all the city in an uproar." —Acts 17:5 NKJV

My Takeaway:

Following God's guidance in the small things changes the big things.

February 7

QUIET TIME NOTES:

- We serve a God who has called us Daughter or Son.
- "I have summoned you by name; you are mine." —Isaiah 43:1
- Until you believe the truth of Scripture in your heart, you will build your life on whatever you value the most.
- God does not calculate our value based on our accomplishments.
- "Well done, good and faithful servant; you were faithful over a few things, I will make you ruler over many things. Enter into the joy of your lord." —Matthew 25:21 NKJV

My Takeaway:

Who we trust is more important than what we do.

February 8

QUIET TIME NOTES:

- Faithlessness stems from self-centeredness.
- "You can't be more like Jesus if you're spending your days staring at all the pictures of who you used to be."
  —Bob Goff, *Live in Grace, Walk in Love*
- God's faithfulness does not change with my mood.
- God has made believing a condition of receiving.
- "Fools find no pleasure in understanding but delight in airing their own opinions." —Proverbs 18:2
- Check your motives: They can easily be stained with self-interest.

My Takeaway:

A self-centered life becomes meaningless.

February 9

QUIET TIME NOTES:

- An algebraic equation we can all understand: GOD > i
- "When you can't stand, He will carry you."
  —St. Francis de Sales
- "Surely I am with you always..." —Matthew 28:20
- "Not was, not maybe, not will be. 'The LORD is my shepherd.'" —Hudson Taylor on Psalm 23:1
- "My times are in Your hand...Make Your face shine upon Your servant..." —Psalm 31:15-16 NKJV
- "My Father, if it is possible, may this cup be taken from me. Yet not as I will, but as you will." —Matthew 26:39

My Takeaway:

Note to my heart: HE > i
(This was tattooed on a woman I met

February 10

QUIET TIME NOTES:

- Being thankful for being forgiven = peace.
- "Blessed is the one whose transgressions are forgiven, whose sins are covered." —Psalm 32:1
- "Let the peace of Christ rule in your hearts…And be thankful." —Colossians 3:15
- "You are able to…consult with God, and change." —Dr. Caroline Leaf, *Switch on Your Brain Every Day*[†]
- The concerns of this world choke our access to Heaven's counsel.

† Dr. Carolyn Leaf, *Switch on Your Brain Every Day*, 2018, Baker Publishing Group.

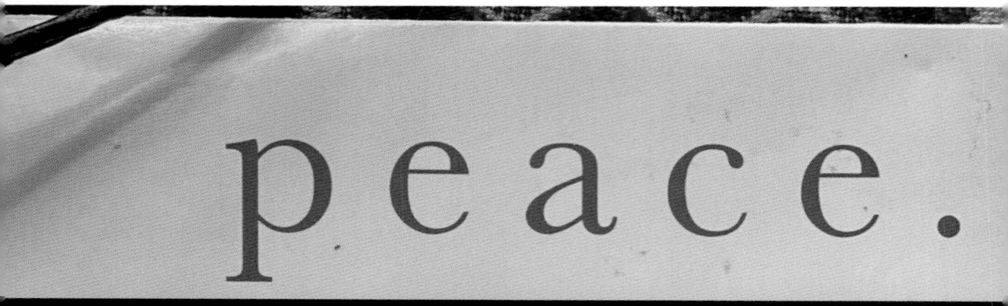

My Takeaway:

Being thankful for being forgiven

February 11

QUIET TIME NOTES:

- Faith in the face of fear removes obstacles.
- Faith that forges ahead will taste triumph.
- "And as soon as the priests who carry the ark of the LORD…set foot in the Jordan, its waters…will be cut off." —Joshua 3:13. (Notice that they set foot in the floodwaters *before* the waters were cut off!)
- Don't wait for the obstacles to be removed in front of you. Faith forges forward.
- "The fear of the LORD is the beginning of knowledge, but fools despise wisdom and instruction." —Proverbs 1:7

My Takeaway:

Trusting God leads to faithful *action*.

February 12

QUIET TIME NOTES:

- We each have a job and a time limit to let God shine through us. He invites us to join His team.
- "No one is to appear before me empty-handed." —Exodus 34:20
- "He fashions their hearts individually; He considers all their works." —Psalm 33:15 NKJV
- The earth on which we walk will someday be dispelled as though it were a mist.
- How I use my time matters; God has set before me good works to do (Ephesians 2:10). Will I choose to do them?

My Takeaway:

Each person has a job and a time limit to let God shine through them.

February 13

QUIET TIME NOTES:

- Grow God, not grief.
- God doesn't send trials to discourage us but to motivate and prepare us for feats we could never do without His help.
- What we plant in our heads sprouts from our hands and mouth.
- "But we have the mind of Christ." —1 Corinthians 2:16
- Do I seek God or his blessings?

My Takeaway:

Free help is available when I focus on God instead of my problem. Grow God, not grief!

February 14

QUIET TIME NOTES:

- Love takes a team. God created us to love Him and each other.
- "For where two or three gather in my name, there am I with them." —Matthew 18:20
- "Haven't you read…at the beginning the Creator 'made them male and female,' and said, 'For this reason a man will leave his father and mother and be united to his wife, and the two will become one flesh.' So they are no longer two, but one flesh? Therefore what God has joined together, let no one separate." —Matthew 19:4-6
- "Above all else, guard your heart, for everything you do flows from it." —Proverbs 4:23

My Takeaway:

God created our hearts to love Him and each other.

February 15

QUIET TIME NOTES:

- God reigns: His magnificent power and plan override ours.
- POTENTATE: A monarch, ruler, or sovereign, especially an autocratic one. One who wields great power or sway.
- "All authority in heaven and on earth has been given to me." —Matthew 28:18
- "May we be alive to every call of duty, accepting without question thy determination of our circumstances..." —Arthur G. Bennett, *The Valley of Vision*
- "Don't be afraid!...He isn't here! He is risen." —Matthew 28:5-6 NLT
- "The righteous person may have many troubles, but the LORD delivers him from them all." —Psalm 34:19

My Takeaway:

The Risen Son reigns. May we bow in awe and adoration of His magnificent power.

February 16

QUIET TIME NOTES:

- In abundance or lack, offer your salty self.
- "For our light and momentary troubles are achieving for us an eternal glory that far outweighs them all." —2 Corinthians 4:17
- Trials do serve a purpose—we have to trust that God is using them for His eternal glory.
- From Leviticus 1:1 to 3:17: The people made… "offerings of the bull…sheep or goats…of birds…of grain…baked in ovens… baked in pans…even covered or uncovered…" My conclusion: Everyone has something to offer, big or small. God honors our gifts to Him.
- "Season all your grain offerings with salt." —Leviticus 2:12 (Make a difference with your love!)

My Takeaway:

In abundance or lack, we are to offer the gift God gives us, seasoned with the salt of ourselves. Don't just go through the motions in life; fully taste it.

February 17

QUIET TIME NOTES:

- Reflecting trust lights our walk home.
- "Now faith is confidence in what we hope for and assurance about what we do not see." —Hebrews 11:1
- It is in the place of the most severe testing, with no apparent way out, that God strengthens our faith.
- God designed us to reflect His image. We are what writer and theologian N.T. Wright calls God's "angled mirrors."
- May God shape and mold me for His service.
- "Righteousness delivers from death." —Proverbs 10:2

My Takeaway:

Rely on God. Reflecting trust lights our path home.

February 18

QUIET TIME NOTES:

- We can choose to love God with a broken heart.

- "Let not our weeping hinder [our] sowing."
  —Arthur G. Bennett, *The Valley of Vision*

- It's easy to become discouraged, but "It is always too soon to give up on God" (Dr. Jim Denison).

- "Love cannot exist without the freedom of choice."
  —Dr. Caroline Leaf, *Switch on Your Brain Every Day*[†]

- "Trust in the LORD and do good...Take delight in the LORD...Commit your way to the LORD...Be still before the LORD and wait patiently for him; do not fret...it leads only to evil." —excerpted from Psalm 37:3-8

† Dr. Carolyn Leaf, *Switch on Your Brain Every Day*, 2018, Baker Publishing Group.

My Takeaway:

Faith chooses to trust, delight, commit, rest, wait, and not fret. We can choose God and continue to be His witnesses, even when our hearts are broken.

February 19

QUIET TIME NOTES:

- Pain positions us to praise with power.
- "Every branch that does bear fruit he prunes so that it will be even more fruitful." —John 15:2
- No one prunes a dead tree. Pruning might produce pain in this world, but it means you're still alive. Make a decision to praise God in the midst of your pruning.
- "He is not far from any one of us. For in him we live and move and have our being." —Acts 17:27-28

My Takeaway:

Perhaps our pain positions us to produce praise, so others may see and awaken to life in Jesus.

February 20

QUIET TIME NOTES:

- "Be still!...Why are you afraid?" —Mark 4:39-40 NLT
- "He is their stronghold in time of trouble. The LORD helps them and delivers them; he delivers them from the wicked and saves them, because they take refuge in him." —Psalm 37:39-40
- If we endure in our times of greatest weakness, sin will lose its power over us.
- "We were created to bring heaven, not hell, to earth." —Dr. Caroline Leaf, *Switch on Your Brain Every Day*[†]
- "Be filled with the Spirit." —Ephesians 5:18
- "'Not by might nor by power, but by my Spirit,' says the LORD Almighty." —Zechariah 4:6

† Dr. Carolyn Leaf, *Switch on Your Brain Every Day*, 2018, Baker Publishing Group.

My Takeaway:

Our silent calm before the Spirit supplies strength.

February 21

QUIET TIME NOTES:

- Trust = no micro-management of God.
- "If you want to get along with God, stay off His throne."
  —Dr. Jim Denison
- "Trust in the LORD with all your heart and lean not on your own understanding." —Proverbs 3:5
- When God makes a promise to us, that means He is present to accomplish it.
- God did not call anyone to the ministry of micro-management.

My Takeaway:

God's promises are absolute. Trust means no micro-management.

February 22

QUIET TIME NOTES:

- Seek forgiveness before you're forgotten.
- We have to confess our sins before God can forgive them.
- "If my people…humble themselves and pray and seek my face…I will hear from heaven, and I will forgive."
  —2 Chronicles 7:14
- "Everyone is but a breath, even those who seem secure."
  —Psalm 39:5

My Takeaway:

My life is but a vapor. I can bow to the Lord on either this side of eternity or the other—but I will bow. God allows me to choose when and where.

February 23

QUIET TIME NOTES:

- My life confirms what I conform to.
- "Do I conform the Word of God to my life, or do I conform my life to the Word of God?" —Pastor Terry Moore, Sojourn Church
- "Do not conform to the pattern of this world, but be transformed by the renewing of your mind. Then you will be able to test and approve what God's will is—his good, pleasing and perfect will." —Romans 12:2

My Takeaway:

I conform to what is most important to me.

February 24

QUIET TIME NOTES:

- Our tasks in life take teamwork.
- "When we droop, revive us. When we loiter, quicken us. When we go astray, restore us." —Arthur G. Bennett, *The Valley of Vision* (Lord, see what I do when left to myself?)
- Am I disgruntled with the assignments God has given me?
- Our task is to reflect heaven on earth.
- One of the hardest things in my life is asking for help—we are not designed to operate on our own.
- "I in them and you in me." —John 17:23 (God does not leave us alone.)

My Takeaway:

The task of living takes teamwork.

February 25

QUIET TIME NOTES:

- My job is to do my work, believing God will do His.
- "I will give you every place where you set your foot."
  —Joshua 1:3 (You possess only what you march across.)
- "The way you live your life is a reflection
  of the way you love your God."
  —Dr. Caroline Leaf, *Switch on Your Brain Every Day*†
- "These people honor me with their lips, but their hearts are far from me." —Mark 7:6
- Wherever you are, that is your kingdom assignment. Embrace it, and God will use this time to strengthen your faith.

† Dr. Carolyn Leaf, *Switch on Your Brain Every Day*, 2018, Baker Publishing Group.

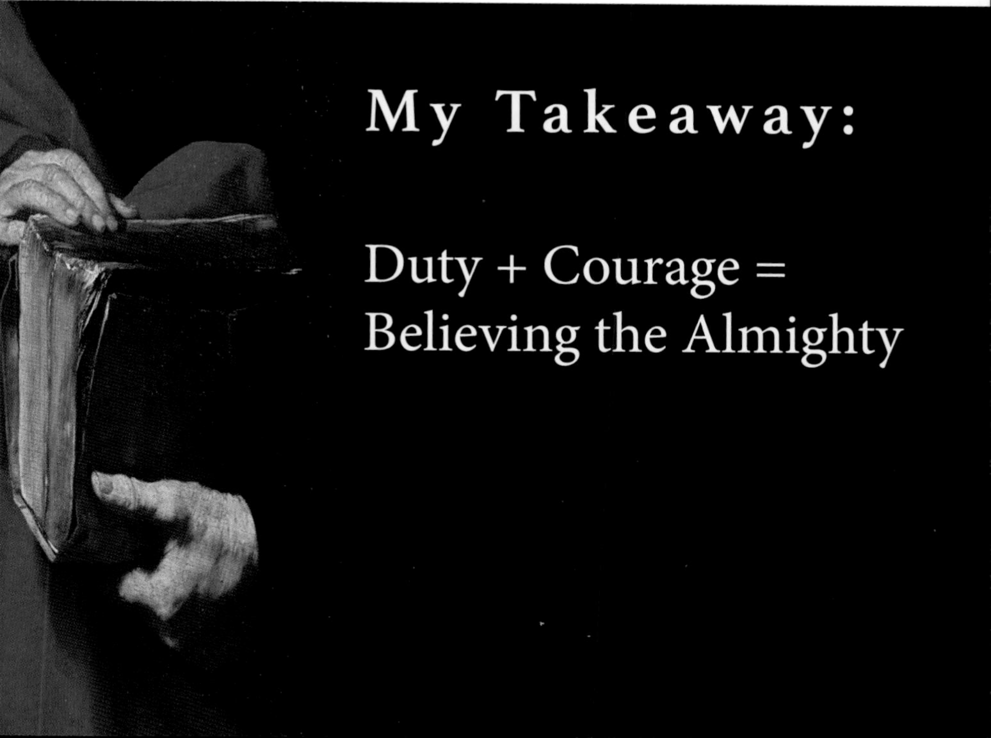

My Takeaway:

Duty + Courage = Believing the Almighty

February 26

QUIET TIME NOTES:

- Be encouraged! God doesn't waste our time. We shouldn't waste it either.
- Don't get so busy saving the world that you fail to see the needs of those closest to you.
- The clock is a merciless master. Stop bowing to busyness.
- "You were running a good race. Who cut in on you to keep you from obeying the truth?" —Galatians 5:7
- "And let us not neglect our meeting together, as some people do, but encourage one another, especially now that the day of his return is drawing near." —Hebrews 10:25 NLT
- This time of repression, oppression, and depression could be a time of training.

My Takeaway:

Be encouraged! God doesn't waste our time. We shouldn't waste it either.

February 27

QUIET TIME NOTES:

- My things can be stolen but not my peace.
- Solomon warns us that there's a "time to gain and a time to lose."
- Happiness doesn't hinge on circumstances. It's all about relying on Jesus in the midst of your circumstances.
- When you're making progress, giants show up.
- "Peace I leave with you; my peace I give you. I do not give to you as the world gives. Do not let your hearts be troubled and do not be afraid." —John 14:27

My Takeaway:

My peace can't be stolen, but my things can. God is so good! Yesterday my purse was stolen, and today He gave me this.

February 28

QUIET TIME NOTES:

- God is not limited by our limitations.
- In Exodus 18, Moses' father-in-law counseled him to get some help instead of doing all the work by himself. This way, Moses could devote himself to the principal task of leading God's people.
- Stay focused on your main work. This is so key to our lives. If even *Moses* needed help with daily distractions to stay focused on his main work, surely we need help to eliminate distractions too!
- Personally, I need to remember the love and provision God freely gives us.

My Takeaway:

God is not limited by our limitations. He will send help when we need it.

March 1

QUIET TIME NOTES:

- A life molded by true worship of God earnestly seeks to serve God.

- You can know about God and not know God.

- "Worship is not the entertainment of man, but the exaltation of God." —Dr. Steven J. Lawson

- "Do every task as though He asked you to do it." —John Piper

- "Whatever you do, work at it with all your heart, as working for the Lord, not for human masters." —Colossians 3:23

My Takeaway:

True worship leads to eternal works

March 2

QUIET TIME NOTES:

- God is in charge. I am not.
- May my character transcend my circumstances.
- “Cutting loose the anchors, they left them in the sea.” —Acts 27:40 (This happened during a storm that ended in a shipwreck, but everyone survived, just as Paul had prophesied.)
- No prayers are lost, but God’s answer might be delayed. He knows when we need to wait. “I called him but he did not answer.” —Song of Songs 5:6
- “Now some of them were in charge of the serving vessels.” —1 Chronicles 9:28

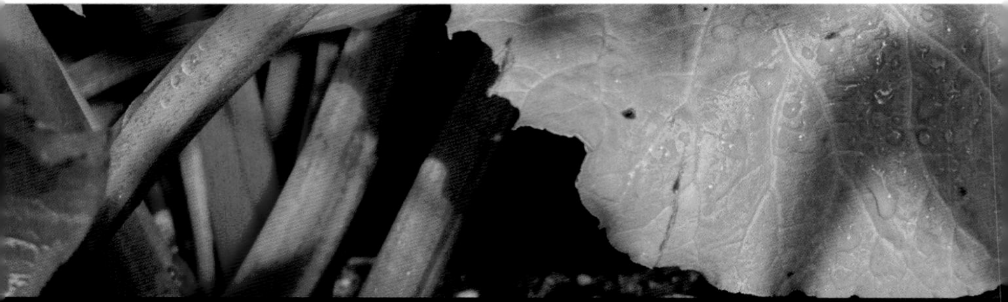

My Takeaway:

My job is to do my job and not try to do God’s. He is in charge and I’m not.

March 3

QUIET TIME NOTES:

- God calls us by name.
- "Do not fear, for I have redeemed you; I have summoned you by name; you are mine." —Isaiah 43:1
- "According to the number of names." (This phrase appears 13 times in Numbers 1:17-47!)
- "I do not trust in my bow…you are the one who gives us victory over our enemies." —Psalm 44:6-7 NLT
- "Come and see what the LORD has done, the desolations he has brought on the earth…He says, 'Be still, and know that I am God; I will be exalted among the nations.'" —Psalm 46:8, 10

My Takeaway:

God knows us by name. We are personal to Him, and He wants our attention so He can give us His Peace.

March 4

QUIET TIME NOTES:

- What do I love most, the gift or the Giver?
- Does our singing stop when the babbling brook dries up?
- "Wait for the LORD." —Psalm 27:14
- Unbelief stifles God's presence.
- "The heinousness of sin lies not so much in the nature of the sin committed, as in the greatness of the Person sinned against." —Arthur G. Bennett, *The Valley of Vision*

My Takeaway:

Do I love the blessings more than the One who bestows them?

March 5

QUIET TIME NOTES:

- Tenacious love tenderly heals us, takes time for us, accepts us, and gives us strength.
- "Love the Lord your God with all your heart, all your soul, all your mind, and all your strength…Love your neighbor as yourself." —Mark 12:30-31 NLT
- Genuine, merciful love heals our minds and bodies.
- To receive great things from God we'll have to persevere through the last and darkest hour.
- "For the entire law is fulfilled in keeping this one command: Love your neighbor as yourself." —Galatians 5:14

My Takeaway:

Love takes tenacity, but it creates a lovely life.

March 6

QUIET TIME NOTES:

- God may be invisible to us, but we are not to Him. Live rightly while you can.
- Lord, in your mercy, help me identify the areas where my heart has grown hard, and give me the courage to allow You to soften them so I can see through eyes of faith once more.
- "In his pride the wicked man does not seek him; in all his thoughts there is no room for God." —Psalm 10:4
- With childlike, joyful trust, expect the next good thing, not the next bad thing.

My Takeaway:

Faith allows us to see God all around us. Spending a moment with God can change your eternity.

March 7

QUIET TIME NOTES:

- Trust God is lighting your path—so you don't end up in a pit.
- If you remove all light, you get total darkness. Similarly, hell is the absence of anything good; it's total badness.
- "Call on me in the day of trouble; I will deliver you, and you will honor me." —Psalm 50:15
- "The ransom for a life is costly, no payment is ever enough—so that they should live on forever and not see decay." —Psalm 49:8-9
- "They will take nothing with them when they die." —Psalm 49:17

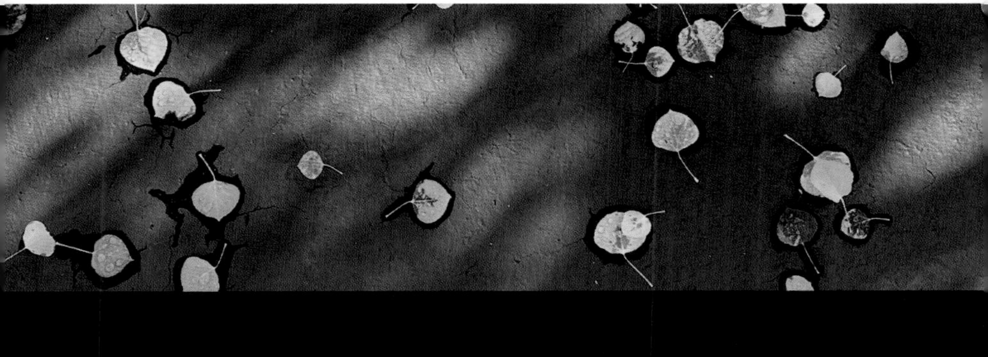

My Takeaway:

When we are lost, our darkness is very dark. But God freely lights the

March 8

QUIET TIME NOTES:

- God is timeless. My "life-quakes" are not.
- God is without beginning or end.
- Stop struggling for your salvation and place your trust in our good and gracious God.
- Trust beyond doubt as you cross your Red Sea. There is no age in eternal life.
- Follow God into your future through your "life-quakes."
- "For God so loved the world that he gave his one and only Son, that whoever believes in him shall not perish but have eternal life." —John 3:16

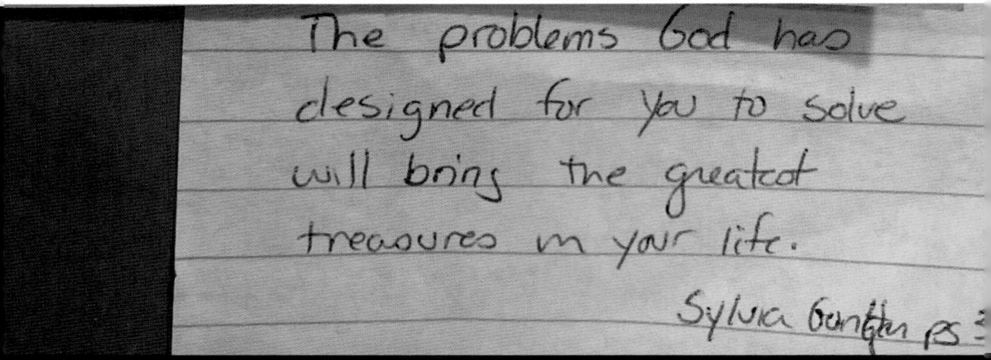

My Takeaway:

God is timeless. Our trials are not. Follow Him into your future.

March 9

QUIET TIME NOTES:

- Exodus 30 contains a lesson from an oil recipe. God gave Moses the recipe for holy anointing oil and sacred incense: It's written out for all to see (Exodus 30:22-25). Then He immediately tells us that it's not for our personal use—it's holy, and if we make some for ourselves, we'll be cut off.

- We know that God told all of this to the Israelites, but we can extrapolate it to the present day. Our bodies are the temple of the Holy Spirit and must be kept holy (1 Corinthians 6:19-20). They were not designed for common use. Yet God allows us to choose what we do with our bodies.

- My realization from this is that God trusts us! He gives us the benefit of the doubt. I find this incredible, as I know how untrustworthy I can be! Yet, He trusts each of us every day to be a channel of His love to others. We can only be trustworthy when His nature is in us, as He is eternally trustworthy.

My Takeaway:

Only through Christ can we embody God's nature.

March 10

QUIET TIME NOTES:

- Be afraid of indifference to God.
- "What good is it for someone to gain the whole world, yet forfeit their soul?" —Mark 8:36
- My life will only serve God if I feel my indebtedness to God.
- It's the law of the farm: You can't fake a harvest.

My Takeaway:

Be afraid of indifference to God. Faith requires courage.

March 11

QUIET TIME NOTES:

- Our presumptuous plans push God aside.

- "But the person who does *anything* presumptuously...he has despised the word of the LORD..." —Numbers 15:30-31

- "Wealth is worthless in the day of wrath, but righteousness delivers from death." —Proverbs 11:4

- "Nothing in you that has not died will ever be raised from the dead." —C.S. Lewis

- Live as though you are on the edge of eternity.

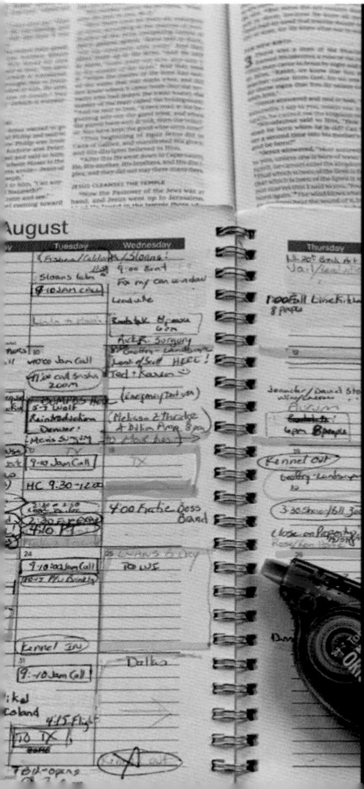

My Takeaway:

Our presumptuous plans need to die so we can actively love and trust God.

March 12

QUIET TIME NOTES:

- God can handle our need. Our future doesn't stress him out.
- There are no five-year plans in Scripture.
- Abraham was "fully persuaded that God had the power to do what he had promised." —Romans 4:21
- Nothing we ask is greater than God is able to give.
- "The greater our need, the greater our need for God." —Dr. Jim Denison

My Takeaway:

God can handle our need. Our future doesn't stress Him out.

March 13

QUIET TIME NOTES:

- Faith's furnace devours fear.
- "When times are good, be happy; but when times are bad, consider this: God has made the one as well as the other. Therefore, no one can discover anything about their future." —Ecclesiastes 7:14
- "Sometimes your greatest blessings come from your most negative circumstances. Let your emotions subside before you decide." —*The Word for You Today*
- Three times Paul was shipwrecked, and three times he survived, according to 2 Corinthians 11:25.
- Perhaps a shipwreck is needed before we trust the compass leading us straight through the Refiner's fire—so He can purify our hearts.

My Takeaway:

Faith burns up fear.

March 14

QUIET TIME NOTES:

- The headline in *The Wall Street Journal* today as COVID-19 hit hard: "The Week the World Shut Down."
- "If you do not stand firm in your faith, you will not stand at all." —Isaiah 7:9
- Times of crisis show us how much we need each other.
- "Dear friends, let us love one another, for love comes from God." —1 John 4:7
- "God isn't dazzled when we go across the ocean.
  He delights when we go across the street."
  —Bob Goff, *Live in Grace, Walk in Love*

My Takeaway:

Dazzling love crosses the street. Doing good makes a difference.

March 15

QUIET TIME NOTES:

- Quarantines force quiet: May we finally see what's important.
- May our hearts shed the insulating layers of daily routines—of things that lull and distract us—and of the numbing surplus of our possessions.
- Creation sees what we can't—and obeys.
- "Then the Lord opened Balaam's eyes, and he saw the angel of the Lord…The donkey saw [him] and shied away…" —Numbers 22:31-33 NLT
- "Tangible help can give eternal hope." —Kevin East, Mentoring Alliance

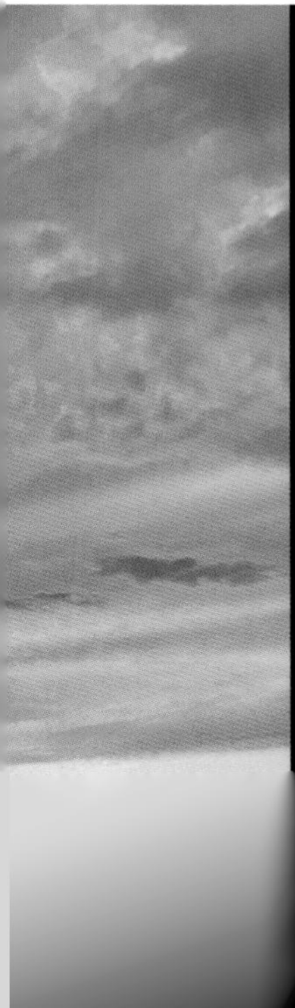

My Takeaway:

I hope you take time today to be alone with God. Our world is in His hands, so we don't have to deal with a crisis alone. God is depending on us to depend on Him.

March 16

QUIET TIME NOTES:

- The way out of a crisis is lit by faith.
- When you come to a beautiful canyon's edge, remember it was birthed in trauma.
- "Now for a little while you may have had to suffer grief in all kinds of trials...so that the proven genuineness of your faith...may result in praise." —1 Peter 1:6-7
- We meet God when we are desperate enough to surrender control.
- "And God said, 'Let there be light,' and there was light." —Genesis 1:3
- "Every crisis in a person's life exposes the gap between what they believe and how they act." —Pastor Joe Martin Jr., C3 Trinity Church

My Takeaway:

The way out of the canyon is lit by faithful praise.

March 17

QUIET TIME NOTES:

- Our hearts long for freedom that has already been granted.
- St. Patrick served as a slave to an Irish farmer before he became a servant of God.
- "He has sent me to proclaim freedom for the prisoners and recovery of sight for the blind." —Luke 4:18
- "When we sin, we choose another way instead of His way." —Daily Briefing, Fellowship of Christian Firefighters International
- We are like a little kid with a shiny coin, worrying about life while ignoring our wealthy Father who desires to take care of our every need.

My Takeaway:

God gives us freedom that we often ignore. Our hearts long for freedom that has already been granted.

March 18

QUIET TIME NOTES:

- Our heart motive matters more than the amount we give.
- "Is trusting God a religious platitude rather than a life-changing attitude?" —Mary Southerland
- "Create in me a pure heart, O God, and renew a steadfast spirit within me." —Psalm 51:10
- "Remember this: Whoever sows sparingly will also reap sparingly, and whoever sows generously will also reap generously. Each of you should give what you have decided in your heart to give, not reluctantly or under compulsion, for God loves a cheerful giver." —2 Corinthians 9:6-7
- God doesn't see our troubles as trials; they are opportunities to grow in trust.

My Takeaway:

Our heart motive matters more than the amount we give.

March 19

QUIET TIME NOTES:

- Strong love seeks, shares, serves: Strong love heals.
- "If my people, who are called by my name, will humble themselves and pray and seek my face and turn from their wicked ways, then I will hear from heaven, and I will forgive their sin and will heal their land."
  —2 Chronicles 7:14
- "Let us not love with words or speech but with actions and in truth." —1 John 3:18
- Strong love braces us for powerful storms.
- Serving others heals the mind and smothers fear. So make a choice: fear or helping others.
- God gives seed to sowers, not hoarders.
  —*The Word for You Today*, my paraphrase

My Takeaway:

Strong love seeks God, shares all, and serves others.

March 20

QUIET TIME NOTES:

- God cuts the chains of fear.
- "Sovereign Commander of the universe, I am sadly harassed by doubts, fears [and] unbelief." —Arthur G. Bennett, *The Valley of Vision*
- The enemy is after the part of God that is inside me, and to get it he'll attack body and mind, planting doubts and fears.
- "Do not be afraid of what you are about to suffer...Be faithful...I will give you life as your victor's crown." —Revelation 2:10
- "Those who dragged their chains shall dance and sing." —*Gates of Repentance*
- "There is surely a future hope for you, and your hope will not be cut off." —Proverbs 23:18

My Takeaway:

God cuts our chains, not our future.

March 21

QUIET TIME NOTES:

- God is the composer and conductor of my Life.
- I trust my composer: He has composed the score of my life, and He is using me as His instrument. I need to trust my composer-conductor!
- My life has one purpose: to bring God honor and glory.
- Have courage. God planned you.
- I give myself to God so He can give Himself to me.
- I have no right to myself. I need to sign sin's death certificate in my life.
- "I will trust and not be afraid…The LORD is my strength and song." —Isaiah 12:2

My Takeaway:

Trust my conductor. He will orchestrate my life for the best song.

March 22

QUIET TIME NOTES:

- It's what we do with fear that frees us. Prayer birthed in distress defines true faith.

- "All degrees of mercy arise from several degrees of prayer." —Arthur G. Bennett, *The Valley of Vision*

- "I removed the burden from their shoulders; their hands were set free from the basket. In your distress you called and I rescued you." —Psalm 81:6-7

- We can endure a short, sharp pain, but prolonged suffering suffocates faith.

- The best way to get a healing boost is to help someone else in pain.

- It's what we do with our fear that defines our faith.

My Takeaway:

Prayer birthed in distress defines true faith.

March 23

QUIET TIME NOTES:

- There is no shortcut through a painful wilderness but to follow God's path.

- "Yet if we choose to follow the Messiah, we… [create] little Edens wherever we live." —Dr. Caroline Leaf, *Switch on Your Brain Every Day*†

- If we persevere through the pain we don't understand, suffering will give way to victory.

- "See, I am doing a new thing!…I am making a way in the wilderness and streams in the wasteland." —Isaiah 43:19

- "There [in the wilderness] you saw how the LORD your God carried you, as a father carries his son." —Deuteronomy 1:31

- "What we do to love and serve our Creator will endure long after we are gone." —C.S. Lewis

† Dr. Carolyn Leaf, *Switch on Your Brain Every Day*, 2018, Baker Publishing Group.

My Takeaway:

There is no shortcut through this wilderness wasteland but to follow God.

March 24

QUIET TIME NOTES:

- God stays close even when we self-isolate from Him.
- Lord, I need not self-isolate from you!
- "We had no rest, but we were harassed at every turn—conflicts on the outside, fears within." —2 Corinthians 7:5
- "He knows you are trudging through this great wilderness." —Deuteronomy 2:7 NKJV
- "Your anxiety decreases as your understanding of God increases." —Greg Laurie
- "The battle you are in will soon nourish your soul." —Os Hillman

My Takeaway:

God doesn't isolate Himself—He stays close to us even when we isolate ourselves from Him.

March 25

QUIET TIME NOTES:

- My eternity depends on a word from Jesus' heart, not on my own words.
- When I realize Jesus came to deliver me from the heredity of sin and I refuse to be adopted by Him, I condemn myself for eternity...The very nature of sin is self-centered.
- "Light came into the world, but people loved the darkness more than the light, for their actions were evil." —John 3:19 NLT
- "In prayer, it is better to have a heart without words than words without a heart." —John Bunyan

My Takeaway:

My eternity depends on a word from Jesus' heart, not on my own words.

March 26

QUIET TIME NOTES:

- Praise is the key to a life of peace.
- Giving God praise is my most important work in life.
- Life is not fair: Good and bad things happen to both good and bad people.
- Rather than always planning, practice trusting God first.
- God is my constant supply.
- The moment I accept forgiveness, my past vanishes. I only have a future. Hallelujah!
- "Give unto the LORD the glory due unto his name…the LORD will bless his people with peace." —Psalm 29:1 & 11 KJV

My Takeaway:

Giving God praise, no matter what happens, is the only thing I can control. Peace comes out of praise.

March 27

QUIET TIME NOTES:

- What I seek is not of this world.
- Jesus said, “My kingdom is not of this world. If it were, my servants would fight to prevent my arrest…” —John 18:36
- Think about where you are spiritually. God calls you to go deeper with Him.
- Countless things fight for my attention. Am I searching for something I can’t grasp?
- It’s not what God gives me; it’s the Giver Himself who is the ultimate gift.
- Job 28:5 says that bread comes from the earth. God provides everything for us, but Job 28:12-19 says that wisdom cannot be bought even for the finest gold.

My Takeaway:

What I’m searching for is not of this world. The greatest gift is the Giver Himself!

March 28

QUIET TIME NOTES:

- Trusting Jesus lights my way.
- Even on (*especially* on) stressful days, Jesus can be trusted.
- Just as you must choose a paint color in the true light of the room, your best life is lived illuminated by Christ's light.
- Whatever I need to do to fulfill God's plan for me today, He'll light the way if I trust Him.
- "You will keep in perfect peace those whose minds are steadfast, because they trust in you." —Isaiah 26:3

My Takeaway:

Trusting Jesus lights my way.

March 29

QUIET TIME NOTES:

- Live expecting God to Help.
- God has provided all that I need. My job is to stand firm.
- Live courageously. Persevere each day.
- Seek God to be my guide. Live expectantly; be ready.
- "In this world you will have trouble. But take heart! I have overcome the world." —John 16:33
- "He shall call upon me, and I will answer him: I will be with him in trouble; I will deliver him, and honor him." —Psalm 91:15 KJV

My Takeaway:

Live expecting God to help you. He has already won the war!

March 30

QUIET TIME NOTES:

- God's fire forces change: Let it burn away your fear.
- Forget your fears; focus on your Father.
- Our minds naturally default to darkness. Deliver me, Lord!
- We can't be a new creation if our thoughts remain the same.
- "The fear of the LORD is the beginning of knowledge." —Proverbs 1:7

My Takeaway:

God's fire forces change: Let it consume our fear.

March 31

QUIET TIME NOTES:

- Our presumptions prevent God's presence.
- "Now the man who acts presumptuously and will not heed the priest...shall die." —Deuteronomy 17:12 NKJV
- God cares more about whether we love than whether we perform well.
- God's expectations are bigger than our own.
- God can't lead us if we won't admit we need to be led.
- God begins where man ends. God frees us when we are caged inside ourselves.

My Takeaway:

Our self-centered presumption that performance matters prevents God's presence.

April 1

QUIET TIME NOTES:

- God doesn't wait until we're dead to give us eternity—He gives it now to keep us from dying.
- "Everything is present tense to Him in eternity."
  —Sylvia Gunter
- "For those who exalt themselves will be humbled, and those who humble themselves will be exalted." —Luke 14:11 NLT
- Have you opened every room of your life to the Holy Spirit?
- "Eternal life is not a gift from God; eternal life *is* the gift of God." —Oswald Chambers, *My Utmost for His Highest*

My Takeaway:

God doesn't wait until we're dead to give us eternity—He gives it now to keep us from dying.

April 2

QUIET TIME NOTES:

- It takes enormous effort to put others before myself, but that effort is my life's purpose. God hears our heartfelt prayers for others.
- When we're climbing a mountain, we're more conscious of our weakness than our progress.
- It's not what I do. It's what I am because of Christ.
- Do I use my gifts to serve others?
- I am a worker under His power. As His child, I can call on Him.
- "Don't look out only for your own interests, but take an interest in others, too." —Philippians 2:4 NLT

My Takeaway:

God gives us His love to share, and we are to pray sincerely for the people He puts in our lives.

April 3

QUIET TIME NOTES:

- I can't fake it with God. Jesus came to melt and mold me, to save me from myself.
- What is replacing God in my life?
- God holds me accountable if I'm not completely yielded to Him.
- Don't be fooled by appearances: The Bible says that "What is seen is temporary, but what is unseen is eternal" (2 Corinthians 4:18).
- "Therefore, if anyone is in Christ, he is a new creation." —2 Corinthians 5:17 NKJV
- Grace empowers us to be transformed.

My Takeaway:

Jesus came to melt and mold me, to save me from myself.

April 4

QUIET TIME NOTES:

- Soul mending takes time, honesty, and awe.
- Slow down; be restored.
- He makes me lie down, He leads, He restores, He guides, He anoints, He cares (Psalm 23).
- Not all miracles happen in a flash. Let His Spirit touch the things that have wrecked me.
- Abject remorse comes from grasping whom we've offended.
- Grace = God's Riches at Christ's Expense
- "Quiet! Be still!" (Mark 4:39). It was spoken to the sea, but perhaps it's meant for me.

My Takeaway:

Slow down and be restored.

April 5

QUIET TIME NOTES:

- Choose others over self.
- Even the souls nearest together need Christ as an interpreter.
- Each soul is different.
- Jesus could have hopped off the cross as God's Son, but He stayed put as a man to save us.
- Jesus chose us over Himself.
- "May God the Father and our Lord Jesus Christ give you grace and peace. Jesus gave his life for our sins, just as God our Father planned, in order to rescue us from this evil world in which you live." —Galatians 1:3-4 NLT

My Takeaway:

Choose your soul friend over yourself.

April 6

QUIET TIME NOTES:

- Trust God's total acceptance.
- We live in front of the open door that Christ made with the cross.
- Gratitude pushes out negative thoughts.
- Stand confident, singled out, wholeheartedly accepted, as a bride before her groom.
- Trust implicitly, based on God's good character.
- "No good thing does he withhold from those whose walk is blameless." —Psalm 84:11

My Takeaway:

I praise God knowing that I'm wholeheartedly loved like a bride standing at the back of the church. Christ opens the doors for me to meet my heart's desire: total acceptance in Him.

April 7

QUIET TIME NOTES:

- Soft clay takes less work.
- My headstrong ways push God out. Am I like cement in His hands?
- Talk to Jesus about your life, relax in His hands, be soft.
- "We are the clay, and you are the potter. We all are formed by your hand." —Isaiah 64:8 NLT
- Like a potter who forms clay, let the Spirit transform your mind.
- "Do not conform to the pattern of this world, but be transformed by the renewing of your mind." —Romans 12:2

My Takeaway:

Allow God to form your thoughts. Be soft clay.

April 8

QUIET TIME NOTES:

- When I believe God, He quiets my soul.
- Don't underestimate the sin of unbelief. It is the reason why Israel wandered in the wilderness for 40 years (Hebrews 3:19).
- "In repentance and rest is your salvation, in quietness and trust is your strength." —Isaiah 30:15
- The secret of knowing God's complete sufficiency is in coming to the end of everything in ourselves.
- The resurrection changes everything.
- "The Spirit of God, who raised Jesus from the dead, lives in you." —Romans 8:11

My Takeaway:

Realizing that God died to live in me changes everything.

April 9

QUIET TIME NOTES:

- Expectations vs. unconditional love: my choice each day.
- Trust God enough to drop your expectations.
- God has an indissoluble union with us!
- Don't ignore God—He's invested His very life in you.
- Forgiveness isn't based on my worth but Christ's.
- "Arise, shine, for your light has come, and the glory of the LORD rises upon you." —Isaiah 60:1
- Do I ignore God to focus on my expectations?

My Takeaway:

Lord, help me to shine in your indissoluble love. Help me to trust your plan for my life.

April 10

QUIET TIME NOTES:

- Sing your one song well.
- God designed each bird with one particular song.
- The stepping stones to heaven are made of obedience.
- The floor of heaven is a mosaic of pure love and joy. Pride blocks the way.
- Make the decision to obey Jesus, not your pride.
- Proclaim the praises of Him (1 Peter 2:9).
- "I will praise you, LORD, with all my heart; before the 'gods' I will sing your praise." —Psalm 138:1

My Takeaway:

Sing the praise song God gave you—don't pretend to be some other bird!

April 11

QUIET TIME NOTES:

- If I fight the pilot, I'll crash.
- The Holy Spirit cannot live as a guest in me, corraled into one room. He invades all of me!
- Don't complain. God designed your day and circumstances.
- Live in this moment; not in your past, not in your future. Live now!
- God's plan pilots me through the storms.
- "This is the day the Lord has made. We will rejoice and be glad in it." —Psalm 118:24 NLT

My Takeaway:

Give God the keys to "me." He is the engineer and pilot. He knows your exact location this day and where He wants you to go. If you fight the pilot, you'll crash.

April 12

QUIET TIME NOTES:

- I need saving from myself. Let me never lose sight of my need for a savior!
- My identity is not my circumstances, my job, my hobbies, or my health. My identity is my love for Jesus.
- Great bumper sticker: If God is my co-pilot, I'm in the wrong seat.
- Do I thrive on conflict or peace?
- "The wisdom from above is first of all pure; then considerate, submissive...willing to yield to others."
—James 3:17 (two translations combined—NIV & NLT)

My Takeaway:

Do I submit to Jesus or myself?

April 13

QUIET TIME NOTES:

- Merge and take the overpass.
- God didn't leave us alone. Jesus wants to be our friend in practical ways.
- Merge your thoughts with Jesus' thoughts about your sins.
- Merge like in traffic: one lane.
- God doesn't see us as deserving of judgment once we merge. He sees one lane—Christ's lane. It serves as both a bridge and overpass—like Passover!
- "Christ, our Passover Lamb, has been sacrificed for us." —1 Corinthians 5:7 NLT

My Takeaway:

Merge. Take the overpass offered and be saved from an eternal traffic jam that won't let you get home.

April 14

QUIET TIME NOTES:

- Praise balances your load.
- Be equally yoked with Jesus! When two people are equally yoked to Christ, their strength multiplies and their sense of purpose intensifies.
- Take one end of Christ's yoke and pull together. Praise Him!
- "Take my yoke upon you and learn from me." —Matthew 11:29
- "If your life is producing only a whine, instead of the wine, then ruthlessly kick it out." —Oswald Chambers, *My Utmost for His Highest*

My Takeaway:

Join your life with Jesus and praise Him as He helps you balance your load.

April 15

QUIET TIME NOTES:

- Each day I choose either God's calmness or my own anxiety.
- Whoever sees the invisible can do the impossible (words from a persecuted Christian).
- Concentrate on a few things until they are accomplished.
- Nothing is an insignificant detail to God.
- Grace overrides karma. I get more than I put out.
- True humility doesn't make you think less of yourself. It makes you think of yourself less.
- "Humble yourselves…under God's mighty hand, that he may lift you up in due time. Cast all your anxiety on him because he cares for you." —1 Peter 5:6-7

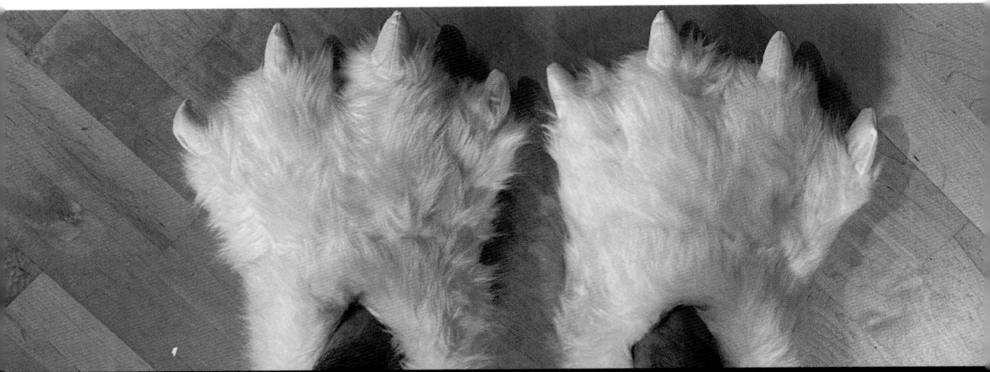

My Takeaway:

Each day, I choose either God's calmness or my own anxiety.

April 16

QUIET TIME NOTES:

- Today's adversity advances my faith.
- "I have given you authority…to overcome all the power of the enemy." —Luke 10:19
- "The righteous will come through trouble." —Proverbs 12:13 NKJV
- Flee from discouragement as from a snake.
- "If you falter in a time of trouble, how small is your strength!" —Proverbs 24:10
- "Comfort and prosperity never enriched the world as much as adversity has." —Billy Graham
- "Each day is a new battle to say yes to what matters and say no to what doesn't." —James Clear, jamesclear.com

My Takeaway:

Today's adversity gives authority to my faith.

April 17

QUIET TIME NOTES:

- Hard question: Why am I resigned to "doing it myself"?
- Am I expressing love for God when I refuse His help?
- Total surrender is reached internally, not externally: It happens in our heart, not our hands.
- I fail to live up to my convictions each day, yet God promises: "I will strengthen you and help you" (Isaiah 41:10 NLT).
- "When I called, you answered me; you greatly emboldened me." —Psalm 138:3

My Takeaway:

Why don't I surrender to God's help? Why am I resigned to "doing it myself"?

April 18

QUIET TIME NOTES:

- Is Jesus inconvenient? At this very moment, is He my Savior—or something less?
- Time is a present God gives us *now*.
- Do I push truth aside when it's inconvenient?
- We can't store up peace for tomorrow. It's like manna.
- Live ready for a surprise visit from God.
- Ask for help, because God holds nothing back. Jesus gave His all.
- "See, I am doing a new thing! Now it springs up; do you not perceive it? —Isaiah 43:19

My Takeaway:

At this very moment, is Jesus my Savior?

April 19

QUIET TIME NOTES:

- We have freedom through the righteousness that comes only from Jesus Christ.

- Jesus knows the names of all the demons He battled from the cross—at one time they were His friends, His angels. He was betrayed not just on a human level, but on a spiritual one, too.

- "For God did not spare even the angels who sinned. He threw them into hell." —2 Peter 2:4 NLT

- Jesus' last words, "It is finished," mark the beginning of freedom for us from the law that we cannot keep. Jesus conquered demonic powers, He disarmed the spiritual rulers and authorities, He shamed them publicly by His victory over them on the cross (Colossians 2:15). He covered us in grace.

- "For he bore the sin of many, and made intercession for the transgressors." —Isaiah 53:12

My Takeaway:

I am righteous through Jesus' sacrifice; He died for my freedom.

April 20

QUIET TIME NOTES:

- Who do I trust in the space between tragedy and triumph?
- All the world's hate couldn't nullify Jesus' love.
- The wounds of friends are the worst.
- Jesus had steadfast belief in God's love, even when all seemed hopeless while hanging on the cross.
- The greatest hope I have is that God continually offers grace to me.
- "He will never leave you nor forsake you." —Deuteronomy 31:6

My Takeaway:

Who do I trust between tragedy and triumph? Jesus trusted His Father even as He hung on the cross.

April 21

QUIET TIME NOTES:

- Each of us should seek to be an influencer to the people in our life—not to thousands of strangers.
- "You are a gift from Him to all the people in your circle of influence." —Sylvia Gunter
- Are you exercising dominion where you have influence?
- "Jabez cried out to the God of Israel, 'Oh, that you would bless me and enlarge my territory!'" —1 Chronicles 4:10 (Perhaps this is more about people's hearts than a land grab.)
- "Then Joshua blessed them…and they went to their homes." —Joshua 22:6

My Takeaway:

Put your effort into being an influencer to the people in your life—not to thousands of strangers.

April 22

QUIET TIME NOTES:

- I get to choose or refuse to be in Jesus' family.
- God sees my heart as only a parent can.
- When I give God control of me, He gives me his unlimited care and love. I become a child who's loved and cared for.
- When I choose Jesus, God seals me with His Holy Spirit, marking me with His eternal ownership and permanent family protection.
- "I am ascending to my Father and your Father, to my God and your God." —John 20:17
- "And he has identified us as his own by placing the Holy Spirit in our hearts as the first installment that guarantees everything he has promised us." —2 Corinthians 1:22 NLT

My Takeaway:

Jesus tells us we are family. We have the same Father—blood ties—and are marked with God's permanent seal.

April 23

QUIET TIME NOTES:

- In the darkest night, God gives us his tent for protection. Stay in the tent.
- May I confide in God.
- I am "lodged in a body like a shepherd in his tent." —Arthur G. Bennett, *The Valley of Vision*
- Even in the darkest times, God has made stars to shine.
- You can be afraid of what you face, or encouraged because God is with you.
- "For the battle is not yours, but God's." —2 Chronicles 20:15
- "For God has not given us a spirit of fear and timidity, but of power, love, and self-discipline." —2 Timothy 1:7 NLT

My Takeaway:

While in the battle, camp in God's tent.

April 24

QUIET TIME NOTES:

- Fear often shows up as excessive planning. Don't plan it. Just live it out.
- Godly deeds take effort.
- Don't just talk about God. Live Him out in front of others.
- "Whatever your hand finds to do, do it with all your might." —Ecclesiastes 9:10
- Love others unrehearsed.
- Prayer is humble reliance on God.

My Takeaway:

Gentle, spontaneous love takes effort. Don't plan it. Just live it. Fear often manifests as excessive planning.

April 25

QUIET TIME NOTES:

- Who or what I trust is obvious to others.
- “The man who reaches the mountain height by the help of train or car has learned no climber’s lesson.” —A.J. Russell, *God Calling* (Lessons take effort.)
- If our relationship is right with God, we’ll do our best regardless of how we feel.
- “Focus on Jesus so I don’t fall when I spin.” —Sarah Young, *Jesus Calling*
- “All you need to say is simply ‘Yes’ or ‘No’; anything beyond this comes from the evil one.” —Matthew 5:37
- “We are therefore Christ’s ambassadors.” —2 Corinthians 5:20

My Takeaway:

Whether I honor my commitments shows who or what I trust.

April 26

QUIET TIME NOTES:

- Relax, stop a moment, and just listen to God. He makes the opportunities and the work.
- Ceaseless activity is not part of God's plan for us.
- Remain true to God, and He will lead you.
- Be willing to give up your own opinions and listen to Him!
- View troubles from an eternal perspective. It simplifies and clarifies them.
- "What is seen is temporary, but what is unseen is eternal." —2 Corinthians 4:18
- If you belong to God, you will be able to hear what He says.

My Takeaway:

Relax and listen for God's guidance.

April 27

QUIET TIME NOTES:

- Believe God wants to bless us when we worship Him.
- "The greatest need we have is not to do things, but to believe things." —Oswald Chambers, *My Utmost for His Highest*
- "Hear and give ear: Do not be proud…Give glory to the LORD your God before He causes darkness, and before your feet stumble." —Jeremiah 13:15-16 NKJV
- "These wicked people, who refuse to listen to my words… and go after other gods to serve and worship them, will be… completely useless!" —Jeremiah 13:10

My Takeaway:

Believe God wants to bless us when we worship Him.

April 28

QUIET TIME NOTES:

- Forgiveness allows His light into my soul.
- God's power flows freely into those who know their need of Him.
- My spiritual perception becomes clearer as I seek forgiveness.
- Darkness and Light cannot coexist.
- "I will be with you." —Exodus 3:12 (God knows we can't do life alone!)
- God gives us individualized love. It's part of His continual quest to track down souls.
- "If you forgive those who sin against you, your heavenly Father will forgive you. But if you refuse to forgive others, your Father will not forgive your sins." —Matthew 6:14-15 NLT

My Takeaway:

Knowing my need for forgiveness allows His light into my soul.

April 29

QUIET TIME NOTES:

- God's light dries up my foggy, misdirected trust in myself.
- I cannot see myself as God sees me.
- The light of His face is the best light by which I can see and assess my life.
- God gives His gifts naturally, like the light from a candle. We don't have to beg to see Him; He's all around us.
- Live in breathless expectation! When we stop expecting surprises from God, it demonstrates that we are trusting only our belief about Him, not actually believing *in* Him.
- Jesus said: "Don't let your hearts be troubled. Trust in God, and trust also in me." —John 14:1 NLT

My Takeaway:

Allowing God's light into my heart dries up my troubles like rays of sun on the morning dew.

April 30

QUIET TIME NOTES:

- Everyone has troubles. Troubles turn us to God, who gives *hope.*
- Believe your life is full of good promises: God says so.
- "And it was very good." —Genesis 1:31
- My failings turn me to God.
- "Consider it pure joy…whenever you face trials." —James 1:2
- "Be kind to everyone, because everyone is having a hard time." —a quote from an elderly professor
- Wholehearted reliance on God is my only hope. Hope is stronger than my performance.

My Takeaway:

Everyone has troubles. Troubles turn us to God, who gives *hope.*

May 1

QUIET TIME NOTES:

- I choose God or myself each day.
- My life is intertwined with the lives of others. A delay from God in my life may be for another's benefit.
- Don't let moments slip away half-lived.
- God will honor your choice whether or not you go to heaven. You don't get there by chance. So do what God asks you to do.
- "Set your mind on things above, not on earthly things." —Colossians 3:2
- "Return to me, for I have redeemed you." —Isaiah 44:22

My Takeaway:

Each day I choose to live fully alive in God's presence or in my own spotlight. Who am I serving?

May 2

QUIET TIME NOTES:

- Jesus, take my hand so I don't get lost.
- Tiny acts of trust bring Jesus closer.
- Whisper His name and He will come closer!
- "Come close to God, and God will come close to you."
  —James 4:8 NLT
- "The prayer of a righteous person is powerful and effective."
  —James 5:16
- "Above all, love each other deeply...Each of you should use whatever gift you have received to serve others."
  —1 Peter 4:8, 10

My Takeaway:

Jesus, take my hand so I don't get lost.

May 3

QUIET TIME NOTES:

- The real blessing in life is Christ in my heart. I am but a mist.
- Kneeling before Christ changes my perspective.
- "You cannot serve both God and money." —Matthew 6:24
- Lord Jesus, please guard and guide us as we are stewards of your blessings.
- "I pray that out of his glorious riches he may strengthen you with power through his Spirit in your inner being, so that Christ may dwell in your heart through faith." —Ephesians 3:16-17

My Takeaway:

The real blessing in life is Christ in my heart!

May 4

QUIET TIME NOTES:

- Love requires action.
- "Let us not love with words or speech but with actions and in truth." —1 John 3:18
- "In all labor there is profit, but idle chatter leads only to poverty." —Proverbs 14:23 NKJV
- "I seek from Him what I could never achieve without Him." —Dr. Jim Denison
- Where you spend your time says a lot about what you value.

My Takeaway:

Love takes action to be proven real. My actions reveal my heart.

May 5

QUIET TIME NOTES:

- We offer our heart to God when we open it to others.
- God has not called me to wall off my heart from others but to be considerate of the details of their lives.
- "Each of you should give what you have decided in your heart to give, not reluctantly or under compulsion."
—2 Corinthians 9:7
- Bring all kinds of offerings to the Lord. (All over Leviticus Chapters 3-9.)
- We have an enormous responsibility to pray for a wicked world (from a persecuted Christian).

My Takeaway:

We offer our heart to God when we open it to others.

May 6

QUIET TIME NOTES:

- Giving our worries more attention than we give to God incapacitates us.
- Legalism will incapacitate you—because rules of man have no power to transform your life.
- "So many things clamor for our focus but few truly deserve it. The Lord is worthy of nothing less than our undivided attention." —Dr. Charles Stanley
- "I'd have gone insane from worry, but my soul believed the truth of God's promises." —George Mueller
- "He will instruct them in the ways they should choose." —Psalm 25:12

My Takeaway:

Giving our worries more attention than we give to God keeps us incapacitated.

May 7

QUIET TIME NOTES:

- Praise during pruning is a powerful witness.
- It's more important to persevere in praise than in petitions. Praise takes our eyes off of our struggles and points us to God.
- Sometimes it's easier to engage in frenetic activity than hold our peace.
- "Hurt feelings don't often want to cooperate with holy instructions." —Lysa TerKeurst
- Trust the Master Gardener: He's a precise pruner.
- "But Jesus remained silent." —Matthew 26:63

My Takeaway:

Praise during pruning is a powerful witness.

May 8

QUIET TIME NOTES:

- God will help me be effective.
- God must direct my effort for me to go forward unafraid.
- Listen and rest in God's plan.
- Self-reliance must be put to death in me by God's power.
- Focus on trusting God and doing what needs to be done.
- "For I am the LORD your God who takes hold of your right hand and says to you, 'Do not fear; I will help you.'" —Isaiah 41:13
- "Be rich in good deeds, and be generous and willing to share." —1 Timothy 6:18

My Takeaway:

It takes faith and effort to be effective not by self-strength but God's strength

May 9

QUIET TIME NOTES:

- Christ powers my life to serve others. Plug into Him!
- Humility is not the belittling of self; it's forgetting self and remembering God.
- Don't flounder in past mistakes. I'm human and I mess up.
- With Christ in me, I am responsible to transform the arena in which I live.
- "For in Christ all the fullness of the Deity lives in bodily form, and in Christ you have been brought to fullness. He is the head over every power and authority." —Colossians 2:9-10
- "The kingdom of God is within you." —Luke 17:21 NKJV
- Be ready to let go of a lesser desire for the sake of a greater life.

My Takeaway:

It takes God in me to serve others.

May 10

QUIET TIME NOTES:

- Love like God does—without fear.
- People don't need your opinion; most of them need love!
- "Do not be afraid; do not be discouraged. Go out and face them tomorrow and the LORD will be with you." —2 Chronicles 20:17
- Love is actually consciousness of God—every day and with everyone.

My Takeaway:

Love like God does—without fear. It will change your world.

May 11

QUIET TIME NOTES:

- Through our troubles we learn to trust God.
- "Our identity in Christ is not determined by our deeds, but displaced by our deeds." —Pete Briscoe
- "You will seek me and find me when you seek me with all your heart." —Jeremiah 29:13
- "Then they cried out to the LORD in their trouble, and he delivered them from their distress." —Psalm 107:6
- The people who have rest and peace achieved it through conflict and pain. They learned to suffer well.

My Takeaway:

God allows storms in our life to teach us to trust His help.

May 12

QUIET TIME NOTES:

- His whisper says, “I’ve got this. Listen to me.”
- Victory means having love, joy, and peace in the midst of the storm. Let “It is well with my soul” be your praise and your cry of faith.
- His voice is gentle and easy to ignore. Attune your ears!
- “Do not be anxious about anything.” —Philippians 4:6
- “…My Presence will go with you.” —Exodus 33:14
- I need a new way of living. Let Him drive.

My Takeaway:

He’s whispering. Listen to Him. He is offering peace.

May 13

QUIET TIME NOTES:

- Throw all your problems on the cross. Let your Savior save you.
- Never judge motives. You can't see the whole picture like God does. Focus on your position as God's child.
- It's about who I belong to, not what belongs to me.
- Truly believing we are God's children gives us power orphans don't have.
- "Humble yourselves, therefore, under God's mighty hand, that he may lift you up in due time. Cast all your anxiety on him because he cares for you." —1 Peter 5:6-7

My Takeaway:

Throw your problems on the cross, and let your Savior save you.

May 14

QUIET TIME NOTES:

- Family life requires God's strength.
- Family members have permission to ask each other for help.
- It is adversity that allows us to exhibit Christ's life in us.
- Refuse to live by self-strength.
- "For with God nothing will be impossible."
—Luke 1:37 NKJV
- "After starting your new lives in the Spirit, why are you now trying to become perfect by your own human effort?"
—Galatians 3:3 NLT

My Takeaway:

God's work requires grace, especially in our families.

May 15

QUIET TIME NOTES:

- Pray, listen, act.
- Spiritual things first, material things second.
- Time alone with God is not a luxury. It's essential.
- I did nothing to achieve salvation, but I must rise to the occasion to show my faith. Prove it.
- Abraham's faith was made complete by what he did (James 2:23).
- Faith can't be just lip service—it must employ hands, heart, head, and feet.
- Key point: We are here to submit to His will and to nourish others.
- For when I was hungry, thirsty, a stranger, needed clothes, sick, and a prisoner, you looked after me (Matthew 25:35-36, paraphrased).

My Takeaway:

Don't just *think* about others. *Pray* for them, and do what your prayer heart says. Pray, listen, act.

May 16

QUIET TIME NOTES:

- Pray and trust who made you. Bring glory to Him, not yourself.
- Prayer re-creates things.
- Think and determine what to do at this moment. Realize that Jesus is right next to you, then do it.
- Self-pity removes God from the throne of my life.
- Am I building my own little kingdom or God's kingdom?
- "May he grant your heart's desires and make all your plans succeed. May we shout for joy when we hear of your victory." —Psalm 20:4-5 NLT

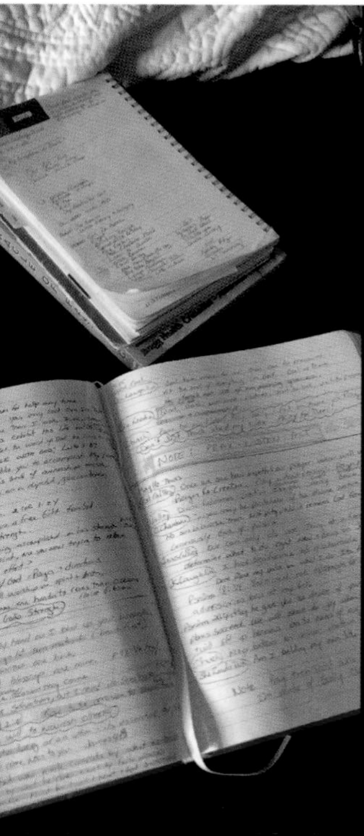

My Takeaway:

Prayer keeps me off God's throne.

May 17

QUIET TIME NOTES:

- He has proved that hard work is worth it.
- "But as for you, be strong and courageous, for your work will be rewarded." —2 Chronicles 15:7 NLT
- "For we are God's handiwork, created in Christ Jesus to do good works." —Ephesians 2:10
- "He who began a good work in you will carry it on to completion." —Philippians 1:6
- You can't succeed without facing adversity. We all reach the point where we're discouraged and want to quit, and how we respond proves the content of our character.
- "Do you see someone skilled in their work? They will serve before kings." —Psalm 22:29

My Takeaway:

Christ did everything needed to accomplish His work. Do likewise to be His true follower it's worth it!

May 18

QUIET TIME NOTES:

- Father knows best. Talk to Him and listen to Him.
- Live today quiet in His love and strong in His power.
- Focus on Jesus. He will make your life matter.
- Don't follow habits. Lord, help me to shun a careless way of life.
- Live in awe, live in His presence, and live in His protection.
- My power, peace, and joy are directly related to the amount of time I spend in prayer.
- "He has shown you, O mortal, what is good. And what does the LORD require of you? To act justly and to love mercy and to walk humbly with your God." —Micah 6:8

My Takeaway:

Father knows best.
Let Him father me.

May 19

QUIET TIME NOTES:

- God gives our pressures a powerful purpose.
- Never make the masses your model.
- Abigail counseled David, do not avenge yourself. (1 Samuel 25—my takeaway.)
- We can be pressed into knowing no helper but God. That's a good thing.
- Weakness always precedes surrender. Quitting isn't an option. The people of Israel had to fight to enter the Promised Land.
- "Now faith is confidence in what we hope for and assurance about what we do not see." —Hebrews 11:1

My Takeaway:

Only God can give our pressures a powerful purpose.

May 20

QUIET TIME NOTES:

- Hard times don't have to harden us. Listen and serve—it's what Jesus did.
- "I am the resurrection and the life. The one who believes in me will live, even though they die." —John 11:25.
- How we react in hard times hinges on where we place our focus.
- Nothing else matters if people feel unwanted.
- People *are* the point.
- We are at our best when we serve others.

My Takeaway:

Hard times don't have to harden our hearts. Listen as Christ did: He heard our cries and came to save us.

May 21

QUIET TIME NOTES:

- When your life seems wrecked, don't doubt in your wilderness. Christ hears our call for help and gives to those who trust Him for victory!
- Don't stay at the entrance of the Christian life. Plunge in.
- Is my first concern Christ or myself? Is doubt my compass, or is faith?
- Don't hijack your own life. Listen and obey God.
- "I wait for God my Savior; my God will hear me." —Micah 7:7
- "I am coming soon. Hold on to what you have, so that no one will take away your crown. All who are victorious will become pillars in the Temple of my God." —Revelation 3:11-12 NLT

My Takeaway:

Hold fast to God. His plan out of the wreckage and wilderness is best.

May 22

QUIET TIME NOTES:

- God gave me His house key.
- Deep intimacy with God is only through His Word, by His Spirit.
- "God's love has been poured out into our hearts through the Holy Spirit, who has been given to us." —Romans 5:5
- I can destroy myself, but I cannot save myself.
- There is no need to knock on God's door. It's open! Know and believe you are family.
- "I in them and you in me." —John 17:23
- Do I live in the house? Or do I wander the streets?

My Takeaway:

God gave us Himself. He adopted us into His family—*nothing can undo that.*

May 23

QUIET TIME NOTES:

- I drop my pile of worries when I focus on eternity with Jesus.
- It's the pile of little things that trips me up: May I never be too busy to attend to my soul.
- Run the "errands" God assigns to you, then report back to Him when done.
- "Do not worry about your life." —Matthew 6:25
- It's not the devil who trips us up. Jesus says it is the "cares of this world" (Matthew 13:22).
- "He who sits on the throne will shelter them with his presence." —Revelation 7:15
- "Love each other as I have loved you." —John 15:12

My Takeaway:

Christ's love brings everything into focus.

May 24

QUIET TIME NOTES:

- I don't have to pretend with God. He already knows all of me.
- He knows where roads will lead, and I don't.
- It is the passing on of our provisions that brings abundance!
- First fruits must be given first. Obey God in this. He knows what you put first.
- "He will be the sure foundation for our times, a rich store of salvation and wisdom and knowledge; the fear of the LORD is the key to this treasure." —Isaiah 33:6

My Takeaway:

God will help me as I obey Him.

May 25

QUIET TIME NOTES:

- God will help me as I talk to Him.
- God waits for me to notice Him. He will stand in the background until I call.
- Realize that God wants the best for you. Exercise your right to waive your rights and let God make the choice for you.
- It is an enormous privilege to kneel before the all-powerful Father and know that He listens and answers!
- When I trust myself over trusting God, I lose joy and peace.
- "The righteous person may have many troubles, but the LORD delivers him from them all." —Psalm 34:19

My Takeaway:

If I listen and follow His guidance, God will help me.

May 26

QUIET TIME NOTES:

- True trust in God develops through the trials He untangles for us.
- Fruitful branches are the ones that attract the attention of the Pruner.
- Be no more afraid than a little girl who places her tangled skein of wool in the hands of a loving mother and runs out to play—with unquestioning confidence in her ability to untangle it.
  —A.J. Russell, *God Calling*, my paraphrase
- One way God redeems suffering is by using it to inspire gratitude.
- Serve God through the suffering. You will emerge grateful for all He has done.

My Takeaway:

True trust comes through trials.

May 27

QUIET TIME NOTES:

- Toil for true treasures.
- “All hard work brings a profit, but mere talk leads only to poverty.” —Proverbs 14:23
- Words alone won’t produce success. You must pray, think, act.
- “All the treasures of a million worlds could not make me richer…for His unsearchable riches are mine.”
  —Arthur G. Bennett, *The Valley of Vision*
- If God gave us Jesus, how will He not give us all we need?
  —Romans 8:32, my paraphrase

My Takeaway:

Our work is to come to Him for life’s true treasures.

May 28

QUIET TIME NOTES:

- I've lived blind while enjoying the sunlight. God sees what I cannot see.

- In His presence you can face uncertainty with perfect peace. God answers prayer the best way every time.

- Be certain that God will reveal things to you as necessary and in accordance with His will.

- Like a plant, the higher the growth, the deeper the root must be: "...his greatness no one can fathom" (Psalm 145:3).

My Takeaway:

God's answers give certain peace.

May 29

QUIET TIME NOTES:

- The way through grief is gratitude.

- I only have Scripture today. I needed the purest help with my grief: "For we will surely die and become like water spilled on the ground, which cannot be gathered up again. Yet God does not take away a life; but He devises means so that His banished ones are not expelled from Him."
—2 Samuel 14:14 KJV

- "For God so loved the world that he gave his one and only Son, that whoever believes in him shall not perish but have eternal life." —John 3:16

- Praise God for the cross!

My Takeaway:

Gratitude for the cross gets us through grief.

May 30

QUIET TIME NOTES:

- Either my eternal spirit or my earthly soul is in charge—it can't be both.
- Our spirit is eternal and connects us to God. Our soul consists of the mind, will, and emotions.
- Our body is the physical wrapper. The body and soul need the spirit to live.
- "'My child, get up!' Her spirit returned, and at once she stood up." —Luke 8:54-55
- We need to surrender the "self" to make room for God in our heart.
- God offers Himself, but I often ignore Him thinking, "I've got this."

My Takeaway:

If I let God lead me, my eternal spirit will be in charge. But if I ignore God, my emotional, earthly soul is in charge.

May 31

QUIET TIME NOTES:

- We choose our stamp: save or destroy.
- "We each must choose whose name will be written on our forehead: 'There before me was the Lamb...and with him 144,000 who had his name and his Father's name written on their foreheads.'" —Revelation 14:1
- Let me be what I profess.
- "There will be no rest day or night for those who worship the beast and its image, or for anyone who receives the mark of its name." —Revelation 14:11
- There is no "yes, but" with God. Know where you are going.
- "The tomb is empty. The throne is not." —Dr. Russell Moore

My Takeaway:

We each must choose: saved forever or burned up.

June 1

QUIET TIME NOTES:

- Do I panic or do I rely on friendship with God?
- The soul is transformed by companionship with Christ.
- It's easier to do something than to trust God. Frenzied activity is evidence of my lack of trust.
- "For I am the LORD your God...Do not fear; I will help you." —Isaiah 41:13
- I choose to worship, rebel, or repent.
- "In your unfailing love you will lead the people you have redeemed." —Exodus 15:13

My Takeaway:

Friends help each other. Do I trust God like I trust a good friend?

June 2

QUIET TIME NOTES:

- Worship saves us from ourselves.
- Preserve me from a false estimate of myself.
- Live in constant awareness of Christ, not just thoughts about Him.
- "For in him we live and move and have our being." —Acts 17:28
- Our natural self shrivels up and dies when we come before God.
- Don't get distracted by the compulsion to perform: Take time to communicate with God and worship.
- "Be still, and know that I am God; I will be exalted among the nations, I will be exalted in the earth." —Psalm 46:10

My Takeaway:

It's worship that saves us from ourselves.

June 3

QUIET TIME NOTES:

- Tiny acts of love pack enormous fear-busting power.
- Love is our most powerful weapon—it opens doors for God to enter.
- Do I leave room for God to talk with me and share His joys?
- It is the tiny things that God helps us with that make us feel most intimate with Him. They show that He knows and cares about all the details of our life.
- "There is no fear in love." —1 John 4:18
- "The only thing that counts is faith expressing itself through love."—Galatians 5:6

My Takeaway:

Watch for God's tiny acts of love. They uniquely show His intimate care for us.

June 4

QUIET TIME NOTES:

- God is courageously faithful to us.
- Through our shortcomings and lack of courage, Jesus tells us: "Surely I am with you always..." (Matthew 28:20).
- No matter how dark your past, the future He has for you is brighter.
- The Spirit of the LORD sets the oppressed free (Luke 4:18, paraphrased).
- "God has never looked in your mirror and wished He saw someone else." —Bob Goff, *Live in Grace, Walk in Love*
- "Only those who will risk going too far can possibly know how far they can go." —T.S. Eliot

My Takeaway:

We can depend on God to get us through if we stay faithful to the call on our life.

June 5

QUIET TIME NOTES:

- Today God gave me deep, stabilizing strength to stand on. In 1 Corinthians 1, Paul writes that we are part of this incredible fellowship in Christ, by grace alone. We're not here because we're the best and brightest—quite the opposite. We are blessed only because He picked us up out of this world and plopped us in His throne room!

  We have access to the Divine, because He chose us. He knows each of us and loves us. But sometimes we don't like the people sitting across the room from us…they bug us.

  Yet Paul shares the biggest "secret" in eternity: The Holy Spirit knows each person's heart, and *He loves them as much as He loves us*. He likes them, even if we don't! With all of our individual differences, we're like a crazy quilt of colors and attitudes. I think that is how He looks at us—each person is beautiful alone, but more wonderful when stitched together with other people, and the more different each person is, the more beautiful the outcome.

My Takeaway:

May the Holy Spirit lock me in life with all kinds of wonderful (and sometimes prickly) people. He chooses each of us, and He knows our hearts, and He knows who needs to sit across the table from us. Trust Him.

June 6

QUIET TIME NOTES:

- I am empty without God.
- I choose to pursue selfish desires to my own detriment.
- I confess that I lack wisdom. I am an empty shell.
- There is no shortcut to holiness. It's gained by spending time in the presence of God, as we receive His unconditional love for us.
- Love, joy, peace, patience, kindness, goodness, faithfulness, gentleness, self-control (the fruit of the Spirit, from Galatians 5:22-23).

My Takeaway:

Only God can fill me with His love.

June 7

QUIET TIME NOTES:

- Faith emerges from struggle.
- Watch out for words without love as you seek your own ends.
- Cut the ties holding you to the dock and push out into the great depths of God.
- Beware of going back to what you once were when God wants to take you where you've never been.
- "Do not cast away your confidence…you have need of endurance." —Hebrews 10:35-36 NKJV
- "Teach us to number our days…establish the work of our hands for us." —Psalm 90:12, 17

My Takeaway:

Cut the ties holding you back. Trust God's promises.

June 8

QUIET TIME NOTES:

- God will touch our lives when we reach out of ourselves.
- "If I can just touch his robe, I will be healed…"
  "Daughter, your faith has made you well." —Mark 5:28, 34 NLT
- "I will display my holiness through those who come near me."
  —Leviticus 10:3 NLT
- You can have as much of God as you want—but the smallness of our minds hinders us!

My Takeaway:

God will touch our lives when we reach out of ourselves.

June 9

QUIET TIME NOTES:

- Only unbelief keeps us undone.
- "Uncertainty is certain."
  —Dana Williams, *The Strengths Journal*
- Pressure and heat will reveal what's really inside us.
- "And because of their unbelief, he couldn't do any miracles among them…And he was amazed at their unbelief."
  —Mark 6:5-6 NLT
- Doubts cause delays. Give thanks in advance for God's promises toward you.

My Takeaway:

Only unbelief keeps us undone.

June 10

QUIET TIME NOTES:

- I can want God most or myself most, but not both.
- On dull days, make deposits into God's great storehouse, little acts of faithfulness that give you something to draw against when in great need.
  —A.J. Russell, *God Calling*, my paraphrase
- "Sacrifice thank offerings to God, fulfill your vows to the Most High, and call on me in the day of trouble; I will deliver you, and you will honor me." —Psalm 50:14-15
- "For everyone who asks receives; the one who seeks finds; and to the one who knocks, the door will be opened."
  —Matthew 7:8
- "The more you fulfill yourself the less you will seek God."
  —Oswald Chambers, *My Utmost for His Highest*

My Takeaway:

Humbly knock on God's door. Desperately and seriously knock.

June 11

QUIET TIME NOTES:

- God loves us in ways we can't understand—He has no limit.
- "You do not realize now what I am doing, but later you will understand." —John 13:7
- "In all things God works for the good of those who love him…" —Romans 8:28
- We are saved by relationship, not rules.
- God's love for us isn't based on our performance, but our specific heavenly reward is.

My Takeaway:

The love God gives us cannot be contained, measured, or even understood—it is the only limitless relationship in our lives.

June 12

QUIET TIME NOTES:

- God lets me choose who or what I worship—and what I choose makes all the difference in the world.
- "We often miss the best in life because we are too busy to worship." —Dr. Tony Evans
- "The LORD tests the heart." —Proverbs 17:3
- God's strength is within us, there for the asking.
- Allow God to light a fire under you. It's not to cause you pain—it's to rescue you from a life without passion.
- "Because they have forsaken the LORD their God… and have embraced other gods, worshiping and serving them—that is why the LORD brought all this disaster on them." —1 Kings 9:9

My Takeaway:

Who or what I worship makes my world worthless or worthwhile.

June 13

QUIET TIME NOTES:

- Listen to those who are loyal to the Lord if you want a lasting legacy. King Rehoboam, Solomon's son, listened to the wrong people and lost it all.
- "Let the wise listen and add to their learning, and let the discerning get guidance." —Proverbs 1:5
- King Solomon wasn't loyal to the Lord, and his successor and son, Rehoboam, rejected the advice of the elders and consulted his young companions instead (based on 1 Kings 11-12).
- "Now get up and go into the city, and you will be told what you must do." —Acts 9:6 (Lord, what do you want me to do?)

My Takeaway:

Seek counsel and listen to those who are loyal to the Lord. Live loyally to leave a legacy.

June 14

QUIET TIME NOTES:

- God uses a chisel when He needs to make the old new.
- Lord, chisel me out of the rock I've been stuck in for so long!
- "See, I am doing a new thing!" —Isaiah 43:19
- There is no, "Lord, wait a minute..." Obey and abide now.
- "I am making everything new!" —Revelation 21:5

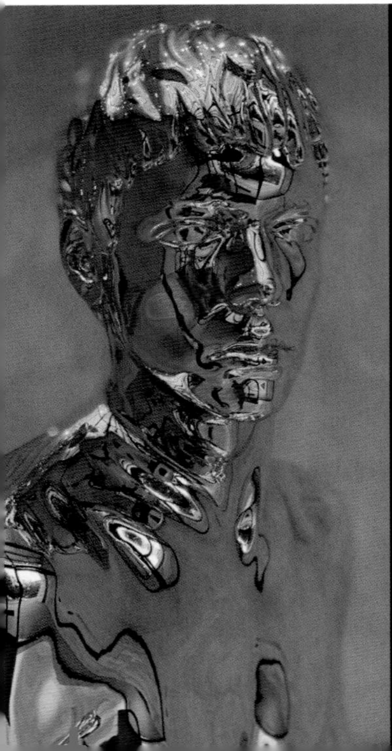

My Takeaway:

Sometimes God must take a chisel to us to uncover the new. Our journey with Him re-creates us.

June 15

QUIET TIME NOTES:

- My troubles are not eternal. Ask the unseen God to fix the problems I can see.
- My greatest snare is myself.
- It is not my circumstances that need altering, but me.
- Today's problem is an opportunity for me to trust God.
- Live in awareness of unseen things, even as we live in a visible world.
- "So we fix our eyes not on what is seen, but on what is unseen, since what is seen is temporary, but what is unseen is eternal." —2 Corinthians 4:18

My Takeaway:

My problems are not eternal. Ask God for unseen help!

June 16

QUIET TIME NOTES:

- To live in peace, do what is right in God's sight.
- "How good and pleasant it is when God's people live together in unity!" —Psalm 133:1
- "I see very clearly that God shows no favoritism. In every nation he accepts those who fear him and do what is right." —Acts 10:34-35 NLT
- "Let all that live revere you. Let them become a single family, doing your will with a perfect heart." (From a Jewish prayer book.)
- We keep our distance from difficult people—exactly the opposite of what Jesus did.

My Takeaway:

Do what is right: Accept others as God has accepted you.

June 17

QUIET TIME NOTES:

- If I ignore God, I'm actually choosing problems.
- Problems are a temporary test of our faith in God. We can choose to remain stuck in our circumstances or endure trouble for a little while and develop character.
- "The testing of your faith produces perseverance. Let perseverance finish its work." —James 1:3-4
- What is our faith if it doesn't produce action?
- Jesus calls us friends. His honor is at stake in my actions.

My Takeaway:

Life is smoother if I choose friendship with God before problems arise.

June 18

QUIET TIME NOTES:

- Trust God with your unknown.

- "Then Peter…walked on the water and came toward Jesus. But when he saw the wind, he was afraid."
—Matthew 14:29-30

- Follow God into the unknown.

- "The steps of a good man are ordered by the LORD."
—Psalm 37:23

- "While we were still sinners, Christ died for us."
—Romans 5:8 NKJV

- Have faith to take the first step.

My Takeaway:

God knows where we are going. Take the first step into the unknown.

June 19

QUIET TIME NOTES:

- Live on purpose. Don't just go through the motions of life.
- Follow the way of obedience. It leads straight to God's throne.
- Am I devoted to Jesus or just to His cause?
- Listening to God is vital to my well-being.
- "A man's heart plans his way, but the Lord directs his steps." —Proverbs 16:9 NKJV
- Out of pain comes purpose.
- Are you running at the end of your endurance? You'll get relief at the foot of the cross.

My Takeaway:

Do I pay attention to my pain or God's purpose for me?

June 20

QUIET TIME NOTES:

- If you want to help yourself, pray for others.
- Unbelief blocks miracles. Miracles require believing faith.
- Intercessory prayer is the key to answered prayer. What we pray for others often returns to us.
- "After Job had prayed for his friends, the LORD restored his fortunes." —Job 42:10
- Realize there are people with bigger problems than yours. Get perspective.
- "You are not your own." —1 Corinthians 6:19
- "The way you store up treasures in heaven is by investing in getting people there." —Rick Warren

My Takeaway:

Praying for others unlocks miracles.

June 21

QUIET TIME NOTES:

- God is not some distant acquaintance—He's your Father and He loves you!
- God allows us to know Him—not as distant admirers but as beloved children!
- "How precious are your thoughts about me, O God…They cannot be numbered." —Psalm 139:17 NLT
- Religion: "I blew it. My Dad is gonna kill me."
  Gospel: "I blew it. I need to call my Dad."
- "The Spirit you received brought about your adoption to sonship. And by him we cry, 'Abba, Father.'" —Romans 8:15

My Takeaway:

God knows us intimately. He gave His Son, and He calls us to receive adoption as His children. Call your Dad—He already knows.

June 22

QUIET TIME NOTES:

- I am guilty of a self-centered, corrupt heart. Thank you, God, for the many prayers You have refused.
- "With the measure you use, it will be measured to you." —Matthew 7:2
- I have no right to judge. I do the same thing I condemn in others. If I cling to Jesus, God judges me against the cross, not my own messed-up heart.
- "You who pass judgment do the same things." —Romans 2:1
- God will bless you to be a blessing to others.
- "From everyone who has been given much, much will be demanded; and from the one who has been entrusted with much, much more will be asked." —Luke 12:48

My Takeaway:

Serving self traps me. I'll get what I give.

June 23

QUIET TIME NOTES:

- God washes off His dirty kids before He lets them in the house. Let Him hose you down.
- God, you know what today holds, and you know what I'm capable of. I ask your blessing and protection from myself.
- Sin upsets our thinking and our plans. Allow God to purify you from all unrighteousness (1 John 1:9).
- There is no greater experience than connecting directly with our Heavenly Father.
- "Blessed are those whose strength is in you, whose hearts are set on pilgrimage." —Psalm 84:5

My Takeaway:

God washes His dirty kids before they walk in the door of His house; amazing

June 24

QUIET TIME NOTES:

- Do I believe God can change me? What and who I believe shapes me.

- God knows the sickness of my heart. Ask for forgiveness and the strength to start again.

- Not recognizing sin produces disasters in my life. Don't compromise with sin!

- "Let us throw off everything that hinders and the sin that so easily entangles. And let us run with perseverance the race marked out for us." —Hebrews 12:1

- "If anyone is in Christ, he is a new creation." —2 Corinthians 5:17 NKJV

- The best protection against indulgence is thanksgiving.

My Takeaway:

What and who I believe shapes me.

June 25

QUIET TIME NOTES:

- Be open in friendships, both earthly and eternal.
- Godly friendships transform your life and make you more like Christ.
- Friendship with God gives life, rest, and shade.
- I can be friends with *the Divine King*. I can call Him and He'll pick up the phone. That is incredible!
- Think of His humble condescension to listen and come to me when I call. I'm just dust!
- He never makes me feel like a waste of His time.
- Sorrow makes us real. You suddenly have time for other people.

My Takeaway:

God wants us unmasked in our friendships, both earthly and eternal.

June 26

QUIET TIME NOTES:

- Life's details determine the outcome.
- Don't give God unprofitable attendance.
- "By what you do in the small things, those around you are more often antagonized or attracted."
  —A.J. Russell, *God Calling*
- Live with precision. Don't slop through life.
- Purpose yields more eternal value than talent.
- He makes me lie down, He leads, He restores, He comforts, He delivers, He answers, He stays with me, He rescues, He honors, He shows His salvation (Psalms 23 & 91).

My Takeaway:

Let God help you with the details of your life. Details determine the outcome.

June 27

QUIET TIME NOTES:

- In the time given, honor God—not self.
- How I use my time determines who I am. Do simple duties well, and success will come.
- Is common sense on the throne of my life, or is God?
- Answer God truthfully: Who is the Master of my life?
- Do I let God handle my P.R., or do I self-promote?
- God designed time to be a protection for us.
- "I am with you and will watch over you wherever you go." —Genesis 28:15

My Takeaway:

Fear God. Use the time He's given you well to bring *Him* honor—not yourself.

June 28

QUIET TIME NOTES:

- Enjoy God's love. It brings joy.
- God has gifted us with joy and gladness for this life. Thankfulness helps us see it!
- The trials of life will crush us if we fail to receive God's love or cultivate communion with Him.
- God's love is not portioned out stingily based on our performance.
- "Taste and see that the LORD is good; blessed is the one who takes refuge in him." —Psalm 34:8

My Takeaway:

Enjoy God's love. It brings joy.

June 29

QUIET TIME NOTES:

- God stays with me through my mess-ups.
- "As I was with Moses, so I will be with you; I will never leave you nor forsake you." —Joshua 1:5
- We face nothing alone. God is with us, whether or not we perceive Him or acknowledge Him. Live as though He is always there—because He is!
- "We are here to glorify God. Nothing else. Life is more about significance than success." —Greg Laurie
- "The LORD makes firm the steps of the one who delights in him." —Psalm 37:23
- "How would past circumstances have turned out differently if only we would have listened to the commandments of God?" —Craig Denison, First15

My Takeaway:

Father knows best. Listen and do what He says. God will stay with me even as He corrects my path

June 30

QUIET TIME NOTES:

- My eternal blessings hinge on the wisdom of sharing my earthly blessings now.
- Let God bring my character to light. "Old too soon, wise too late."
- Will I merely make a living or will I make a difference?
- Pass every blessing on. You will find that treasures await you in the years that lie ahead.
- It doesn't matter if I'm cheated as long as I don't cheat others.
- "But seek first his kingdom and his righteousness, and all these things will be given to you as well." —Matthew 6:33

My Takeaway:

The more I share from my heart, the more I'm blessed.

July 1

QUIET TIME NOTES:

- Don't live life on autopilot. Take time to inhale God.
- The wilderness isn't all thorns and thirst. God is there, and He sees you.
- The key is to trust and be calm in the storm.
- "But this happened that we might not rely on ourselves but on God, who raises the dead." —2 Corinthians 1:9
- We need time alone with God to process our thoughts. Do whatever it takes to carve out this time.
- "Choose to inhale. Do not simply breathe to exist." (These are the last words 13-year-old poet Mattie Stepanek spoke to his mom.)

My Takeaway:

Inhale God deeply and enjoy life.

July 2

QUIET TIME NOTES:

- I woke up late, but I knew I needed at least a moment with God before I attacked my to-do list, so I decided to read Psalm 15.

When I opened my Bible, I saw a note I'd written in the margin years ago. I subtitled this Psalm: "How God Defines Success."

"LORD, who may dwell in your sacred tent? Who may live on your holy mountain?
The one whose walk is blameless, who does what is righteous,
who speaks the truth from their heart; whose tongue utters no slander,
who does no wrong to a neighbor, and casts no slur on others;
who despises a vile person but honors those who fear the LORD;
who keeps an oath even when it hurts, and does not change their mind;
who lends money to the poor without interest;
who does not accept a bribe against the innocent.
Whoever does these things will never be shaken." —Psalm 15

My Takeaway:

The words of this Psalm are such a kind reminder as we are entrusted with God's blessings.

July 3

QUIET TIME NOTES:

- A roadblock can crush you, or you can rely on God to crush it.
- Daniel's three friends would rather die for God than live with the Devil (Daniel 3:16).
- "The human spirit can endure in sickness, but a crushed spirit who can bear?" —Proverbs 18:14
- Approach your roadblocks with faith and confidence. God has your back.
- "Why should I be frightened and surprised by the plow of the Lord, which makes deep furrows in my soul?...He is not some...irrational farmer—His purpose is to yield a harvest." —Samuel Rutherford, *Streams in the Desert*

My Takeaway:

God knows who trusts Him and how to crush our roadblocks.

July 4

QUIET TIME NOTES:

- Small worries are like a mosquito that won't leave us alone.
- "Say to those with fearful hearts, 'Be strong, and do not fear, for your God is coming to destroy your enemies. He is coming to save you.'"—Isaiah 35:4 NLT
- "And let the peace that comes from Christ rule in your hearts…And always be thankful." —Colossians 3:15 NLT
- Swat those mosquitoes with gratitude and childlike faith!
- Prayer and praise take us through our anxieties—to peace!

My Takeaway:

It hurts God's heart to see us anxious.

July 5

QUIET TIME NOTES:

- God forgave me, so why is it so hard for me to forgive others?
- "He lifted me out of the slimy pit…he set my feet on a rock."
  —Psalm 40:2
- "Forgive when it's costly, not just when it's convenient."
  —Bob Goff, *Live in Grace, Walk in Love*
- Do what is best, not what is easy.

My Takeaway:

God forgave me, so why is it so hard for me to forgive others?

July 6

QUIET TIME NOTES:

- True faith, not status, chisels life's hard edges.
- I have believed the false god of self. May I be chiseled from the old rock where I've been embedded for so long.
- Faith often requires us to take our hands off of things only God can fix.
- Give it to God, and stop grabbing it back.
- "We'll be known for our opinions, but we'll be remembered for our love. Don't forget what will matter in the end. The love you leave behind will be your legacy." —Bob Goff, *Live in Grace, Walk in Love*
- "People, despite their wealth, do not endure." —Psalm 49:12

My Takeaway:

True faith, not status, chisels life's hard edges.

July 7

QUIET TIME NOTES:

- Confident courage learned through hard times changes us for the better.
- "In quietness and confidence shall be your strength." —Isaiah 30:15 NKJV
- Rocks get polished after plenty of time in the tumbler.
- A jewel is produced through time, heat, pressure, and precise cutting.
- Build up a reservoir of courage, determination, and good character when life puts you to the test.
- "I have…no loom to weave my own righteousness." —Arthur G. Bennett, *The Valley of Vision*

My Takeaway:

Humble confidence in God is usually found amidst tears.

July 8

QUIET TIME NOTES:

- We all spend many unproductive hours and fall short of God's best for us.
- We don't drift aimlessly into God's will.
- Make God's will your will, and He will guide you.
- I try hard to escape from the Sculptor's hand in an attempt to hammer myself into the shape of my own goals.
- Let the Potter put you on His wheel and whirl you around for a while.
- "He who began a good work in you will carry it on to completion until the day of Christ Jesus." —Philippians 1:6

My Takeaway:

God's excellence takes effort.

July 9

QUIET TIME NOTES:

- God knows our trials today and will lighten our load tomorrow. Trust Him.
- "And because we were exceedingly tempest-tossed, the next day they lightened the ship." —Acts 27:18 NKJV
- "God is a just judge, and God is angry with the wicked every day." —Psalm 7:11 NKJV
- "Each one of us has to be heroic, no matter who we are." —James P. Owen, *Cowboy Ethics*
- God uses trials to shape us into His image.
- You can doubt God if you don't really know Him, but if you know Him as Friend, Savior, and Father, it's definitely wrong to doubt.

My Takeaway:

Trust the trial to eventually lighten your load.

July 10

QUIET TIME NOTES:

- God gives life unleashed.
- “You are my Lord; apart from you I have no good thing…The boundary lines have fallen for me in pleasant places; surely I have a delightful inheritance. I will praise the Lord, who counsels me.” —Psalm 16:2, 6-7
- Live with deliberate commitment: Life requires initiative.
- Every day you’re alive is a gift! Don’t hold back on the love and laughter.
- Will you trust Him?
- Don’t be pretentious with Jesus. He knows you.
- “I have called you friends.” —John 15:15

My Takeaway:

Laugh and love unleashed.

July 11

QUIET TIME NOTES:

- Live beyond the darkness.
- I'm not here for self-realization but to know Jesus.
- "Forget the former things, do not dwell on the past. See, I am doing a new thing!" —Isaiah 43:18-19
- Current idols are more subtle than ancient ones.
- "The LORD turns my darkness into light." —2 Samuel 22:29
- "He drew me out of deep waters." —2 Samuel 22:17

My Takeaway:

God's unseen love and protection are available but often concealed by sneaky idols. So, walk in the light!

July 12

QUIET TIME NOTES:

- It's beyond our understanding: Asking + Believing = Joy.
- God completes every task committed to Him.
- To fulfill God's perfect plan for me, I need to surrender mine.
- I'm not alive to enjoy a quiet spiritual life. I'm alive to know Him and share in His life!
- The power in Jesus' name is beyond our understanding.
- "Until now you have not asked for anything in my name. Ask and you will receive, and your joy will be complete." —John 16:24

My Takeaway:

Asking + Believing = Joy.

July 13

QUIET TIME NOTES:

- Don't rehearse disasters. Relax your mind.
- Live in joyful trust like a child. Expect good.
- God uses external circumstances to bring about internal changes.
- "Put off your old self…be made new in the attitude of your minds." —Ephesians 4:22-23
- Don't live behind a mask, subconsciously letting others require you to perform or conform. Instead of trying to fix yourself, fix your eyes on Jesus. Let Him shape your life.

My Takeaway:

Listen to God whisper in your ear: "I made you the way I wanted you. Relax and enjoy who I made you to be!"

July 14

QUIET TIME NOTES:

- Take the long view. God is eternal, and my problems are not.
- "Whoever sees the invisible can do the impossible."
  —A persecuted Christian
- There is no age in eternal life.
- It is God's honor that is at stake, not mine.
- Pay attention to who you're trying to please with your life.
- Out of pain comes true praise.
- "He turned to me and heard my cry. He lifted me out of the slimy pit…and gave me a firm place to stand." —Psalm 40:1-2

My Takeaway:

God is eternal,
and my problems
are not.

July 15

QUIET TIME NOTES:

- Who or what is holding the top of my ladder?
- My first sin of the day leads into others.
- I've been hasty and short in private prayer. God should withdraw His presence when we relate to Him so carelessly—but He doesn't.
- "You are not your own; you were bought at a price." —1 Corinthians 6:19-20
- Do you pray more for yourself or for others to know the love of Christ?
- If God calls you to climb up, He will hold the top of your ladder.

My Takeaway:

Is my ladder lying flat on the ground or leading me to God?

July 16

QUIET TIME NOTES:

- We still need to obey God's rules for life.
- "Keep my decrees and laws, for the person who obeys them will live." —Leviticus 18:5
- "I have set you apart from the nations to be my own." —Leviticus 20:26
- I'm trudging through the book of Leviticus, which is hard to read because it details a ton of rules against detestable, ungodly things—things that would make your skin crawl. But clearly God needed to establish rules against such behaviors because humans (yes, us) did all those things!

My Takeaway:

Oh Lord, have mercy on us—we still need to obey your rules for life.

July 17

QUIET TIME NOTES:

- Self-effort mangles Christ's love for us.
- I cannot be my own God. Why is this so difficult for me to understand?
- Refuse to be distracted.
- "Most people put Jesus on hold until they have spare time." —Sarah Young, *Jesus Calling*
- We glorify busyness, not Jesus.
- "But one thing is needed, and Mary has chosen that good part, which will not be taken away from her." —Luke 10:42
- Try putting your name in place of Mary's. That makes it personal.

My Takeaway:

My self-centered, scattered efforts won't lead me to God. Only one-on-one focus on Christ will.

July 18

QUIET TIME NOTES:

- God knows each of us by name. He knows my assigned purpose.
- In 1 Chronicles Chapters 24-27, hundreds of people are listed by name with the work assignments God gave them. These hard-to-pronounce names go on page after page. They seemed pointless to me until I realized that everyone is important to God, and He knows the work He's given each of us to do!
- "The LORD looks down from heaven…to see if there are any who understand, any who seek God." —Psalm 14:2

My Takeaway:

God knows me, and He knows my purpose.

July 19

QUIET TIME NOTES:

- We are not alone if we have but a seed of faith. God will water it with courage.
- God has already given us what we need to succeed, but it's in seed form.
- "Rise up; this matter is in your hands. We will support you, so take courage and do it." —Ezra 10:4
- "I will be with you." —Isaiah 43:2
- "Little faith will bring souls to heaven, but great faith will bring heaven to your souls." —Charles H. Spurgeon
- "Put out into deep water." —Luke 5:4

My Takeaway:

We are not alone if we have but a seed of faith. God will water it with courage.

July 20

QUIET TIME NOTES:

- Check which track you are on.
- Knowing right from wrong doesn't make you righteous—only repentance does.
- "Repent, for the kingdom of heaven is at hand!" —Matthew 3:2 NKJV
- "The darkness of the tunnel does not contradict the sovereignty of the engineer driving the train." —Dr. Jim Denison
- Before we ask others to change, we must ask God what needs to change in our own lives.

My Takeaway:

Knowing what is right and living righteously are two different things. Check which track you're on.

July 21

QUIET TIME NOTES:

- Focusing on Christ's wisdom gives us hope.
- "Chasten your son while there is hope…For if you rescue him, you will have to do it again." —Psalm 19:18-19 NKJV
- "Often there is so much emphasis on what is bad for us and what can go wrong that we forget to focus on what is good for us." —Dr. Caroline Leaf, *Switch on Your Brain Every Day*†
- Solomon asked God for wisdom and knowledge that he might rule well. God gave that and much more! (My paraphrase of 2 Chronicles 1:10.)
- "Many are the plans in a person's heart, but it is the LORD's purpose that prevails." —Proverbs 19:23

† Dr. Carolyn Leaf, *Switch on Your Brain Every Day*, 2018, Baker Publishing Group.

My Takeaway:

Praise God for Christ's wisdom available to us! He gives us hope!

July 22

QUIET TIME NOTES:

- Clinging to our old life and ignoring God's directions leads to the wrong answer.

- "We can become spiritually rich if we let the cyclone shake us so that our dry leaves and rotten fruit fall down." —A persecuted Christian

- Follow God's direction obediently, as a child. Live under divine control. Trust Him for the results.

- "For the LORD searches all hearts and understands all the intent of the thoughts. If you seek him, he will be found by you; but if you forsake him, he will cast you off forever." —1 Chronicles 28:9

My Takeaway:

God expects obedience at the heart level.

July 23

QUIET TIME NOTES:

- We can't hide.
- Grant that I may never lose sight of the extreme sinfulness of sin or the extreme righteousness of salvation.
- Be real before Him. The secret me is the real me.
- Time can be a tyrant, but God is timeless. Often the problems around you aren't nearly as urgent as we think they are. Though people will forget you, God never will. Come before God with an unveiled face, as Moses did (Exodus 33:7-11).
- "But whenever anyone turns to the Lord, the veil is taken away." —2 Corinthians 3:16

My Takeaway:

There is nothing we can hide from God.

July 24

QUIET TIME NOTES:

- Quiet hearts trust their Maker.

- "In quietness and trust is your strength." —Isaiah 30:15

- "It was the message from God to His servants in days of anxiety and dire distress. The enemy was at the gate… on every side was feverish unrest and disbelief in the possibility of anything but failure. And God sends to them His prophet. He bids them to trust Him and not fear." —Randall T. Davidson, Dean of Windsor and Domestic Chaplain to the Queen, London, 1885

- Stay close to Jesus. That is the answer to all of our troubles.

- "Does not the potter have power over the clay?" —Romans 9:21 NKJV

My Takeaway:

Quiet hearts trust their Maker while facing trouble.

July 25

QUIET TIME NOTES:

- God sees the possibilities; we see the problems.
- "But as for you, be strong and do not give up, for your work will be rewarded." —2 Chronicles 15:7 NKJV
- We will endure great spiritual upheaval if we obey His words. Have you made a decision to follow Him, come what may?
- God desires to raise us up for a noble purpose: to be everlasting pillars in the palace of His kingdom.
- Focus on your purpose, not your problem.

My Takeaway:

God sees our possibilities; we see our problems.

July 26

QUIET TIME NOTES:

- May I accept that my pride must be destroyed by God or it will destroy me.
- "True patience is expressed when we must even wait *for* hope." —*Streams in the Desert*
- So often we perceive the hand of a foe long before we perceive the hand of God.
- "Though I walk in the midst of trouble…with your right hand you save me." —Psalm 138:7
- "Every fool is quick to quarrel." —Proverbs 20:3

My Takeaway:

My pride thinks my problem is bigger than my Protector.

July 27

QUIET TIME NOTES:

- Be *present* with your grieving friends through pain.
- "And let us consider how we may spur one another on toward love…encouraging one another." —Hebrews 10:24-25
- "Faith is depending on the fact that God loves me, not on my ability to figure out how or why." —Mona Khauli
- "Our God…we have no power to face this vast army that is attacking us. We do not know what to do, but our eyes are on you." —2 Chronicles 20:12
- God continually chooses the ignorant, the fragile, and the broken to express His grace and unconditional love.

My Takeaway:

Show up to hold up your friends—even when you don't know what to do. God will go with you.

July 28

QUIET TIME NOTES:

- He can't fill me when I'm full of myself. I need to come to Him empty.
- We are idolaters by nature.
- "Not to him who walks on, with no obstacles in his way, but to him that *overcometh is the promise given*." —A.J. Russell, *God Calling*
- It's the process—not the outcome—that glorifies God.
- "We are meant to be marked by similarity to the one whom we serve and love…You are not the person you were before salvation." —Craig Denison, First15
- "Do not get drunk on wine…Instead, be filled with the Spirit." —Ephesians 5:18

My Takeaway:

Until I abandon my sinful self, God can't help me or fill me.

July 29

QUIET TIME NOTES:

- Can I come through a cloud without damaging my view of God?
- Let Christ's victory be displayed in your life: "Continue in him, so that when he appears we may be confident and unashamed before him at his coming." —1 John 2:28
- If there were no clouds in our life, we would never develop faith. Clouds in life aren't so much to teach us something as to cause us to *un*-learn something. Thank God for clouds.
- Sunlight eventually pokes through the clouds!
- "...That the love you have for me may be in them and that I myself may be in them." —John 17:26

My Takeaway:

In the end, it's how I handled my clouds that will make me happy (unashamed) as I stand before Him.

July 30

QUIET TIME NOTES:

- Let God wash your soul; cleansing rains come from the darkest clouds.
- The person who's troubling you the most is often revealing the flaws in your own character.
- "His way is in the whirlwind and the storm, and clouds are the dust of his feet." —Nahum 1:3
- "Behold, He is coming with clouds." —Revelation 1:7 NKJV
- We need our clouds. They ultimately simplify our lives.
- "God doesn't often send what we think we need. He sends us what He knows we need." —Bob Goff, *Live in Grace, Walk in Love*

My Takeaway:

Cleansing rains come from the darkest clouds.

July 31

QUIET TIME NOTES:

- Consider your character, because God does.
- It is healthy to study your character and consider where you're entangled in sin.
- "Each of us will give an account of ourselves to God. Therefore let us stop passing judgment on one another." —Romans 14:13
- "God saw all that he had made, and it was very good." —Genesis 1:31
- God will provide ample guidance when we fully trust Him.

My Takeaway:

Consider your character, because God does.

August 1

QUIET TIME NOTES:

- Surrender your sin to the Lord: Pleading ignorance is not an option.
- Sin never surrenders without a fight.
- "You'll miss the best things if you keep your eyes shut." —Dr. Seuss
- "God doesn't need us to do 'great things.' He wants us to do the next right thing." —BreakPoint
- "We will not fear, though the earth give way…[though] nations are in uproar…Be still, and know that I am God." —Psalm 46:2, 6 & 10

My Takeaway:

When we wholeheartedly serve God, He gently shines a light on our sin.

August 2

QUIET TIME NOTES:

- Run the race God sets for you to win the eternal prize.
- Paul said: "I have finished the race…Now there is in store for me the crown of righteousness, which the Lord, the righteous Judge, will award to me…" —2 Timothy 4:7-8
- Am I wasting time on trivial pursuits instead of the one thing God has called me to do?
- "Search me, God…lead me in the way everlasting." —Psalm 139:23-24
- The trials of life build perseverance and strength.

My Takeaway:

Run the race God sets for you to win the prize. Your salvation isn't at stake if you're in Christ, but your heavenly rewards are.

August 3

QUIET TIME NOTES:

- Don't wallow in your wilderness—God's grace provides the way out.
- Help me to see my wilderness for what it is—the place where God refines me so I can step into His Promised Land.
- When I reach the end of my self-sufficiency, I can be of use to God.
- "If my people…will humble themselves and pray…I will hear…and forgive their sin." —2 Chronicles 7:14
- "When you're riding through hell…keep riding."
—James P. Owen, *Cowboy Ethics*

My Takeaway:

Don't wallow in your wilderness—Jesus is the way out.

August 4

QUIET TIME NOTES:

- Prayer makes our work worthwhile.
- Deeds done in the Spirit never die.
- Nehemiah was a cup-bearer, not a carpenter, but God equipped him to rebuild the walls of Jerusalem because he believed and said "yes" to the Lord.
- Nehemiah's prayer came first, then his work. Prayer was not an afterthought.
- God will use us to the degree we trust Him.

My Takeaway:

Prayer is not an add-on to our work—it is our work if we want eternal results.

August 5

QUIET TIME NOTES:

- Self-importance destroys friendship.
- An old saying: "In prosperity our friends know us, but in adversity we know our friends."
- "The one who rules [should be like] the one who serves." —Luke 22:26
- Our own striving destroys the calm God offers. His call is simply to be His friend.
- We forget who we are when we're always in a rush. Slow down for your friends.
- "You are a chosen people…God's special possession, that you may declare the praises of him." —1 Peter 2:9

My Takeaway:

Pay attention to helping (serving) your friend—that's true friendship. Friends help friends.

August 6

QUIET TIME NOTES:

- Jesus fills dried-out souls.
- Times alone with God are necessary for refilling our souls. Oneness with the Lord should be our goal, not quick answers.
- Everyone you meet is fighting a battle in their lives.
- "Do nothing out of selfish ambition or vain conceit. Rather, in humility value others above yourselves." —Philippians 2:3
- Jesus was willing to stop everything to take time for one person.
- "Share with the Lord's people who are in need. Practice hospitality." —Romans 12:13
- "Give us today our daily bread." —Matthew 6:11

My Takeaway:

Only one-on-one time in Christ's love can moisten my dried-out sponge of a soul so I have the capacity to wipe others' tears.

August 7

QUIET TIME NOTES:

- Self-trust insults God.
- Do I trust the shelter God provides in my storm?
- Persistent doubts offend our loving God.
- The Holy Spirit visits by invitation, so invite Him into your prayers.
- God's sovereignty doesn't negate my responsibility!
- "Trust in the LORD with all your heart and lean not on your own understanding." —Proverbs 3:5

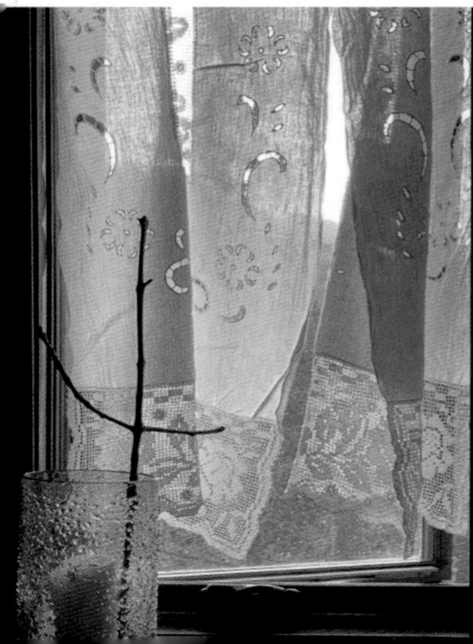

My Takeaway:

My responsibility is to ask, listen, and trust God. Trusting myself pushes Him out of my life.

August 8

QUIET TIME NOTES:

- Reclaiming lost territory doesn't feel like victory, but it is. Trust God and slog on.

- Lord, forgive me for wasted time.

- A drowning man is totally at the mercy of his rescuer. We are helpless. Trust in God completely.

- "For his anger lasts only a moment, but his favor lasts a lifetime; weeping may stay for the night, but rejoicing comes in the morning." —Psalm 30:5 NKJV

- Champions don't feel like champions till a few weeks after the race is over.

- Do I only pray when things go wrong?

My Takeaway:

Reclaiming lost territory doesn't feel like victory—but it will in the end. Trust God on this.

August 9

QUIET TIME NOTES:

- God's rules matter more than manmade rules.
- Supernatural sense is God's gift; common sense produces common results.
- "A person may think their own ways are right, but the LORD weighs the heart." —Proverbs 21:2
- "These people come near to me with their mouth…but their hearts are far from me. Their worship of me is based on merely human rules they have been taught." —Isaiah 29:13
- "The true test of a man's honor was how much he would risk to keep it intact." —James P. Owen, *Cowboy Ethics*

My Takeaway:

Common sense isn't meant to rule our life. Strength of character matters more than manmade rules.

August 10

QUIET TIME NOTES:

- We can be alone—or choose to be with God.
- "But whoever is united with the Lord is one with him in spirit…Do you not know that your bodies are temples of the Holy Spirit, who is in you?" —1 Corinthians 6:17, 19
- "Turn to me and be gracious to me, for I am lonely and afflicted." —Psalm 25:16
- "If you have any encouragement from being united with Christ…being one in spirit and of one mind…value others above yourselves." —Philippians 2:1-3
- God promises to give peace, not pleasure.

My Takeaway:

We can be alone—
or choose to be
with God.

August 11

QUIET TIME NOTES:

- If we give our all to God, He gives His all to us.
- We must accept that God's love allows pain.
- "So when he heard that Lazarus was sick, he stayed where he was two more days." —John 11:6
- We all traverse our own Red Sea. No one can do it for us.
- "If you are unfaithful, I will scatter you among the nations; but if you return to Me…I will gather [you]…for My name." —Nehemiah 1:8-9
- "Return to the LORD your God, for he is gracious and merciful, slow to anger, and of great kindness; and He relents from doing harm." —Joel 2:13 NKJV

My Takeaway:

We all have pain. God promises that if we give our all to Him, He'll give His all to us.

August 12

QUIET TIME NOTES:

- All our doubts and fears melt when met with true belief.
- God's ability to save the world isn't limited by our belief that He can do it.
- Power and guidance are multiplied when two are seeking the one true God.
- Nothing is greater than the Spirit of God living in you: "Christ in you, the hope of glory" (Colossians 1:27).
- "Jesus answered, 'The work of God is this: to believe in the one he has sent.'" —John 6:29

My Takeaway:

All our doubts and fears melt when met with true belief.

August 13

QUIET TIME NOTES:

- God's leading is worth fighting for.
- "Those who carried materials did their work with one hand and held a weapon in the other, and each of the builders wore his sword at his side as he worked." —Nehemiah 4:17-18
- "I will instruct you and teach you in the way you should go; I will counsel you with my loving eye on you." —Psalm 32:8
- Should they decide to believe only in their hearts to escape arrest? —A persecuted Christian
- Does my life line up with Jesus?
- "Whatever your hand finds to do, do it with all your might." —Ecclesiastes 9:10 NLT

My Takeaway:

God expects you to fight for your faith.

August 14

QUIET TIME NOTES:

- It takes audacity to ignore eternity!
- "'Return to me, and I will return to you,' says the LORD Almighty." —Malachi 3:7
- "Here I am! I stand at the door and knock." —Revelation 3:20
- Why aren't we standing on the porch waiting? Why do we make God wait?
- "We need to constantly be knocking on the door in His presence. He wants us to be with Him eternally, but we think life is a game." —Laura B.
- "Jesus Christ is the same yesterday and today and forever." —Hebrews 13:8

My Takeaway:

Answer the door. Don't make eternity wait.

August 15

QUIET TIME NOTES:

- We can live differently if we quiet our heart and listen to His.
- Let's pause our ceaseless activity and give God time to work.
- Don't fill the quiet spaces with our own accusations and expectations.
- "The effect of righteousness will be quietness and confidence forever." —Isaiah 32:17
- God's mercies are renewed each morning (Lamentations 3:22-23). Dwell in that mercy throughout the day.

My Takeaway:

Confidence in God is more powerful than our own accusations. We will live differently if we quiet our heart and listen to His.

August 16

QUIET TIME NOTES:

- We can love Jesus by loving others or ignore Him by ignoring others.
- “We must be purposely kind and generous or we miss the best part of life’s existence.” —Horace Mann
- Do yourself some good: Do good to others.
- “Gratitude fills us, grumbling drains us.” —Richard Swenson, *Margin*
- “No one should seek their own good, but the good of others.” —1 Corinthians 10:24

My Takeaway:

We can love Jesus by loving others or ignore Him by ignoring others. It’s our choice.

August 17

QUIET TIME NOTES:

- Check your baggage at the gate.
- "The world is artful to entrap [with] gilded bait [and] every painted bauble." —Arthur G. Bennett, *The Valley of Vision*
- Jesus doesn't try to lure us in, He stands at the gate calling our name. He opens the gate and never lets us drag our past in with us.
- When we speak Jesus' name and His Word aloud, we open the Eye Gate and the Ear Gate to our soul.
- "Do not fear, for I have redeemed you; I have summoned you by name; you are mine." —Isaiah 43:1

My Takeaway:

His gate is for souls only…no carry-on bags!

August 18

QUIET TIME NOTES:

- Surrender, step aside, and let Him guide.
- I am a traveler on this earth, with a pilgrim's staff in my hand.
- I must surrender my will to God. This is a battle I fight every day!
- Stop ducking difficulties—you're in the hands of the God of the impossible!
- "Whoever dwells in the shelter of the Most High will rest in the shadow of the Almighty." —Psalm 91:1
- "By taking shortcuts—you risk shortchanging your future…God calls prepared people, so prepare yourself." —*The Word for You Today*

My Takeaway:

Everyone—no exceptions—must follow the Leader.

August 19

QUIET TIME NOTES:

- Turning to God turns our fears into hope.
- I can't be my own Christ, and I can't manufacture my healing, hope, or restoration.
- Self-pity is from Satan. Awareness of Christ crowds out self-awareness.
- "The dark clouds hide the sun, but it is not extinguished… Our Lord's love letters often come in dark envelopes." —Charles H. Spurgeon, from *Streams in the Desert*
- "The Lord is not slow in keeping his promise…Instead he is patient with you, not wanting anyone to perish, but everyone to come to repentance…you have been forewarned." —2 Peter 3:9, 17

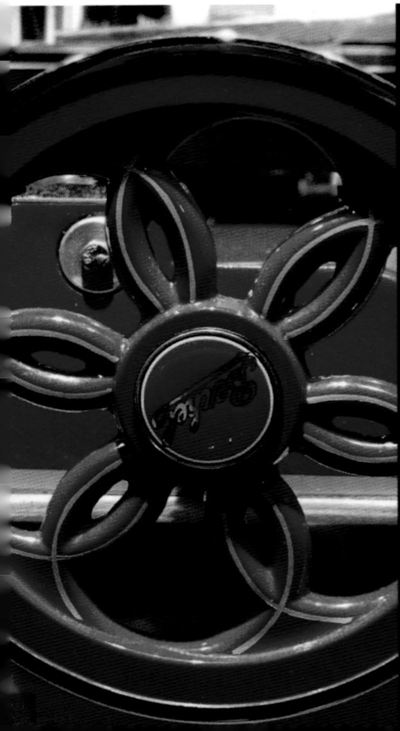

My Takeaway:

We can't give ourselves hope, but God turns our sincere repentance into hope.

August 20

QUIET TIME NOTES:

- I woke up early this morning, and the birds were singing their hearts out. I heard it as worship, and I opened my devotionals to discover this message:

  In God's calmness, He offers us His friendship as we worship Him. He offers us His timetable. He offers us His purpose for our lives. He offers us His healing, His joy, His lordship.

  In addition to all of this, He chooses me to be his bride! To be one with Him, joining Himself with me in my heart and spirit. He gives Himself to me each morning as the birds sing, and each moment of each day. He accepts me as I am, and He makes me His bride. That is inconceivable to me. Yet that is our God! He wants me close. He wants us close, so He comes close to us!

My Takeaway:

Hallelujah. Praise God for His outrageous love!

August 21

QUIET TIME NOTES:

- God's love balances us.
- "Clipped wings can grow again…'Behold, I make all things new.'" —A.J. Russell, *God Calling*
- Receiving the love of Christ to greater and greater degrees brings deliverance.
- "The thing about canoes is this. They're tippy…The tip happens when your center of gravity gets too high. The same is true of us. If our heads are full and our hearts are empty, we'll tip over." —Bob Goff, *Live in Grace, Walk in Love*
- "Love never fails." —1 Corinthians 13:8

My Takeaway:

Self-centered love tips us over—God's love raises us. God-centered love always balances us.

August 22

QUIET TIME NOTES:

- I rightly worry when I think I'm in control.
- A habit of gratitude loosens the ties of control.
- Pray or worry are your two options; worry is an affront to God.
- "So don't worry...your heavenly Father already knows all your needs." —Matthew 6:31-32 NLT
- We carry stress as if we can control things.
- "If we confess our sins, he is faithful..." —1 John 1:19

My Takeaway:

Worry is ignoring God.

August 23

QUIET TIME NOTES:

- God gives each of us a responsibility and the time to accomplish it.
- Specific tribes of Israel had specific responsibilities: some to lead, some to care for the tabernacle, some to care for the sanctuary, and some to bear responsibility for the frames, poles, and other items that supported the holy spaces. Moses and Aaron had final responsibility (Numbers 2).
- A busy life isn't always a productive life. We will give an account for the time God has given us.

My Takeaway:

God gives each of us a responsibility and the time to accomplish it.

August 24

QUIET TIME NOTES:

- Don't let the hard parts of life harden your heart. Trust Him.
- "Take your pains and sufferings, difficulties and hardships… and offer them up…So the beauty of each day will live on after the trouble and distress." —A.J. Russell, *God Calling*
- "From six calamities he will rescue you; in seven no harm will touch you." —Job 5:19
- Your Bible belongs in your heart, not on the bookshelf.
- No matter what happens, we always have the option to love.

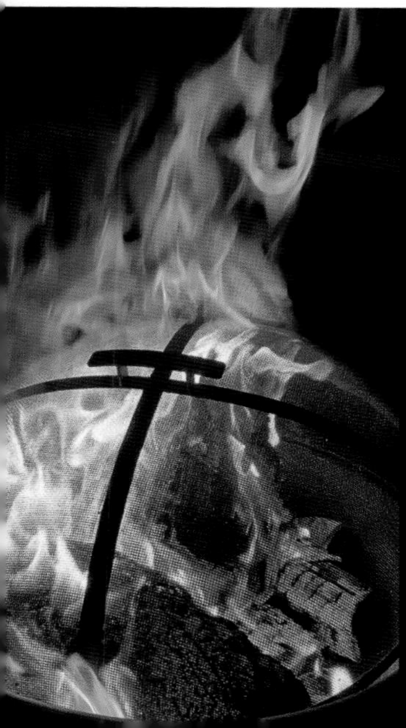

My Takeaway:

Don't let the hard parts of life harden your heart. Trust Him.

August 25

QUIET TIME NOTES:

- You can't just think good thoughts—you actually have to do good things. Take time to pray.
- Good works can't help but overflow from a fervent prayer life.
- May we live so we hear, "Well done, good and faithful servant!" (Matthew 25:21).
- "Create in me a pure heart, O God, and renew a steadfast spirit within me" (Psalm 51:10). This was my first prayer this morning on a well-loved prayer bench a friend gave me. God knew I needed a heart reset!

My Takeaway:

You can't just think good thoughts—you actually have to do good things, and that takes time in prayer.

August 26

QUIET TIME NOTES:

- Prayer widens our path around the debris of wickedness.
- "People who pray aren't special—God is Special."
  —Yang Zhang, a persecuted Christian
- Our sins and weaknesses push us to approach the Throne of Grace. "A broken and contrite heart, O God, you will not despise" (Psalm 51:17).
- God's way is not so narrow that He can't walk beside us.
- "The triumphing of the wicked is short." —Job 20:5

My Takeaway:

Prayer helps us bypass wickedness.

August 27

QUIET TIME NOTES:

- Repentance is a chisel.
- "Those who cleanse themselves...will be instruments for special purposes, made holy, useful to the Master." —2 Timothy 2:21
- "Love is the measure of life; only so far as we love do we really live." —John Burroughs
- There is a constant hammering and sawing going on in the inside as the Holy Spirit works to meet a deadline and make me an instrument for His purposes. —*The Word for Today*, my paraphrase
- "Repent, then, and turn to God, so that your sins may be wiped out, that times of refreshing may come from the Lord." —Acts 3:19

My Takeaway:

When I repent of ignoble living, God chisels me into someone He can bless.

August 28

QUIET TIME NOTES:

- Salvation = Peace

- God's time is very different from ours. "The Lord is not slow in keeping his promise, as some understand slowness. He is patient with you, not wanting anyone to perish, but everyone to come to repentance" (2 Peter 3:9).

- Help me be attentive to my character and concerned about others' salvation.

- God doesn't lower His standards for anyone.

- "You have put gladness in my heart, more than in the season that their grain and wine increased. You alone, O LORD, make me dwell in safety." —Psalm 4:7-8 NKJV

My Takeaway:

Lord Jesus, I ask the safety of your salvation for my family and friends. You alone satisfy me more than the finest earthly treasures. I ask for this gift of peace, in Jesus' Holy Name.

August 29

QUIET TIME NOTES:

- "Scuba" into God's Word to wash away fear.
- When we take hold of God's "righteous right hand" (Isaiah 41:10) like a trusting toddler, all fear melts away.
- God's Word will not return to Him empty (Isaiah 55:11, paraphrased).
- "Who of you by worrying can add a single hour to your life? Since you cannot do this very little thing, why do you worry about the rest?" —Luke 12:25-26 (It amazes me that God thinks adding time is an easy thing!)
- "Motives are weighed by the LORD. Commit to the LORD whatever you do, and he will establish your plans." —Proverbs 16:2-3

My Takeaway:

Am I waterskiing over God's Word or scuba diving into it? Deep-think His promises.

August 30

QUIET TIME NOTES:

- Listen to His song—you are loved unconditionally.
- "The LORD your God is with you…[He] will rejoice over you with singing" (Zephaniah 3:17). Like a mom softly singing a lullaby to her child, God has you in His arms—holding, rocking, caring, and loving you.
- Lord, keep me from running after fleeting pleasures that dissolve into nothing.
- God desires a relationship with us—not service.
- "Love…always perseveres." —1 Corinthians 13:7

My Takeaway:

Listen for His love song today.

August 31

QUIET TIME NOTES:

- Fear leads to damaged lives; faith in God leads to fruitfulness.
- Jesus doesn't look at your past to determine your future. All family trees have bruised fruit.
- "For the Spirit God gave us does not make us timid, but gives us power, love and self-discipline." —2 Timothy 1:7
- "Because you have turned away from the LORD, the LORD will not be with you." —Numbers 14:43 NKJV
- Oh, that we'd desire to have Jesus in us, more than a manmade injection.

My Takeaway:

Fear leads to damaged lives; faith in God leads to fruitfulness.

September 1

QUIET TIME NOTES:

- The only thing that matters in this life is relationship: our relationship with God, and our relationships with others. Everything else can be taken away.
- "How good and pleasant it is when brothers live together in unity!" —Psalm 133:1
- "Let us think of ways to motivate one another to acts of love and good works. And let us not neglect our meeting together, as some people do, but encourage one another..." —Hebrews 10:24-25 NLT
- As we are set to spend the weekend with friends, may we share deep relationships that are truly the beauty of our lives.

My Takeaway:

It pleases God when we put people over projects.

September 2

QUIET TIME NOTES:

- Want God to help you and listen to you? Return the favor.
- Caring for others when we have needs of our own builds resilience when we endure stress.
- "Give, and it will be given to you. A good measure, pressed down, shaken together and running over." —Luke 6:38
- The burdens of others will be lifted to the extent that we share in them.
- "Carry each other's burdens, and in this way you will fulfill the law of Christ." —Galatians 6:2

My Takeaway:

By helping others and listening to them, we ourselves are helped—and heard.

September 3

QUIET TIME NOTES:

- God is already sitting next to your friend—we are not left alone.
- “Two are better than one... Though one may be overpowered, two can defend themselves. A cord of three strands is not quickly broken.” —Ecclesiastes 4:9, 12
- “After Job had prayed for his friends, the LORD restored his fortunes.” —Job 42:10
- “The LORD Almighty is with us.” —Psalm 46:7
- “I will live with them and walk among them.” —2 Corinthians 6:16
- Share life with God—and friends.

My Takeaway:

As we share life with friends, God joins us.

September 4

QUIET TIME NOTES:

- Be humble as you work hard, knowing you need Christ's help.
- Don't carry burdens that were meant to be dropped at the foot of the cross.
- "Do not be over-righteous, neither be overwise—why destroy yourself?" —Ecclesiastes 7:16
- "Whatever your hand finds to do, do it with all your might." —Ecclesiastes 9:10
- We live today, but there is a time limit!

My Takeaway:

Be humble as you work hard, knowing you need Christ's help.

September 5

QUIET TIME NOTES:

- If you are weary, let God build you up again.
- I think it all comes down to truly believing the prayer we whisper.
- God promises us this morning: "I will build you up again" (Jeremiah 31:4).
- The law of heaven is progress, but we must give thanks before it happens.
- Thank the Giver, and the gift will come.

My Takeaway:

"I will build you up again."

September 6

QUIET TIME NOTES:

- We are accountable for our actions. God doesn't bend His rules.
- "Remember the One at whose bar we must both presently appear." —George Whitefield, in a letter to Benjamin Franklin
- "Because of the LORD's great love we are not consumed." —Lamentations 3:22
- "...For God Himself is Judge...Call upon Me in the day of trouble; I will deliver you, and you shall glorify Me. But to the wicked God says: "What right have you to declare My statutes...Seeing you hate instruction? ...And to him who orders his conduct aright I will show the salvation of God." —Psalm 50:6, 15-17, 23 NKJV
- "You must be born again." —John 3:7

My Takeaway:

In the end, we will all be judged by our actions. We are accountable to God, and He doesn't bend His rules.

September 7

QUIET TIME NOTES:

- Live like a colander. Let love flow uninhibited.
- If I stay connected to Jesus, I will never run out of goodness to share.
- He let every ounce of His love flow through to us without self-preservation in mind.
- "Love must be sincere. Hate what is evil; cling to what is good. Be devoted to one another in love. Honor one another above yourselves." —Romans 12:9-10

My Takeaway:

I pray I can live like a colander.

September 8

QUIET TIME NOTES:

- Only by giving of yourself will you gain unbounded happiness. Focus on your source and flow forward.
- I begin my day bowed before Him: "Lord, here is my empty heart."
- Good Shepherd, save me from myself!
- "In the pursuit of happiness, half the world is on the wrong scent. They think it consists in having and getting, and in being served by others. Happiness is really found in giving and serving others." —Henry Drummond (1851-1897), Scottish evangelist, biologist, writer
- Releasing your grip on the past allows you to reach for your future.
- "Forgetting those things which are behind…" —Philippians 3:13 NKJV

My Takeaway:

A river never looks back, it flows forward to new life—do the same.

September 9

QUIET TIME NOTES:

- God works *in* me before he works *through* me.
- "Remember your great field of labor is yourself. That is your first task, the weeding, the planting...pruning, bearing fruit. When that is done, I lead you out into other fields." —A.J. Russell, *God Calling*
- "Woe to those who are wise in their own eyes and clever in their own sight." —Isaiah 5:21
- No matter what you're facing, it's too soon to give up on God. Look to Jesus; He will perfect your faith (Hebrews 12:2).

My Takeaway:

God works *in* me before He works *through* me.

September 10

QUIET TIME NOTES:

- It's scarier to disobey God than anything man can do to you.
- "The opposite of courage isn't fear, it's conformity."
  —*The Word for You Today*
- Be real before God. The secret me is the real me.
  (Note in my Bible.)
- Once God shows you a truth, instantly apply it and live up to it.
- "O God, You know my foolishness; and my sins are not hidden from You." —Psalm 69:5 NKJV
- "Courage has always been at the heart of Christian discipleship."
  —Dr. Jim Denison

My Takeaway:

It's scarier to disobey God than anything man can do to you.

September 11

QUIET TIME NOTES:

- Anxiety has always been with people, but so has God.
- "Come to me…and I will give you rest." —Matthew 11:28
- "Fear and trembling have beset me; horror has overwhelmed me…Destructive forces are at work." —Psalm 55:5, 11
- "Cast your cares on the LORD and he will sustain you." —Psalm 55:22
- "Each generation will lift the fallen to their feet and hold them as they learn to walk. And as they learn to walk, the sickness of our time will be healed by those who drink deep from the ancient wells of truth." —*Gates of Repentance*
- Answering God's call answers our anxiety.

My Takeaway:

God's truth gives our souls rest. It is the answer to our anxieties.

September 12

QUIET TIME NOTES:

- We choose either God's good gifts or gloom.

- "Chances are, if you're feeling disheartened, it's because you are thinking gloomy thoughts. If you want to feel uplifted, make a concerted effort to think uplifting thoughts."
—*The Word for You Today*

- "What I want is not your possessions but you."
—2 Corinthians 12:14

- "The Spirit of the LORD will rest on him—the Spirit of wisdom and of understanding…counsel and of might…knowledge and fear of the LORD." —Isaiah 11:2

- How we handle ordinary things reveals who we truly are.

- "And now, dear brothers and sisters…Fix your thoughts on what is true, and honorable, and right, and pure, and lovely, and admirable." — Phillipians 4:8 NLT

My Takeaway:

Every day we can turn to God's goodness and be uplifted, or choose to stay gloomy.

September 13

QUIET TIME NOTES:

- Faith disinfects discouragement.
- "Depression, gloom, pessimism, despair, and discouragement stop more people than all the world's combined illnesses…You can never be defeated unless you're defeated in your thinking." —*The Word for You Today*
- "Just as the hand, held before the eye, can hide the tallest mountain, so the routine of everyday life can keep us from seeing the vast radiance and secret wonders that fill the world." —Hasidic saying from the 18th century, quoted in Norman Doidge's book *The Brain's Way of Healing*
- "Examine yourselves to see whether you are in the faith; test yourselves." —2 Corinthians 13:5

My Takeaway:

Faith disinfects discouragement. It unveils wonders that have always been there.

September 14

QUIET TIME NOTES:

- Waiting may be disobedience that complicates life.
- "People who spend their lives 'waiting for their ship to come in' are usually disappointed—or die on the pier." —*The Word for You Today*
- We grow under the load we carry, and we build strength when we endure amidst opposition.
- Obedience is the power that simplifies our life.
- "But don't just listen to God's word. You must do what it says. Otherwise, you are only fooling yourselves."—James 1:22 NLT
- "Those who worship false gods turn their backs on all God's mercies." —Jonah 2:8 NLT

My Takeaway:

Waiting in disobedience complicates life.

September 15

QUIET TIME NOTES:

- Hardship intensifies praise. Fear blocks it.
- Beautiful music comes from a minor key. Frankincense is only sweet when scorched by fire. Fruits sweeten when touched by frost.
- Make a decision to praise God regardless of how you feel. When you change your focus, your feelings will change too.
- "Fear is toxic to the brain and body...If we let our fears control us, we will create chaos and disorder in the mind."
—Dr. Caroline Leaf, *Switch on Your Brain Every Day*†
- "For it is...God who commanded light to shine out of darkness."
—2 Corinthians 4:6 NKJV
- "Do not let your hearts be troubled and do not be afraid."
—John 14:27

† Dr. Carolyn Leaf, *Switch on Your Brain Every Day*, 2018, Baker Publishing Group.

My Takeaway:

Hardship intensifies praise. Fear blocks it.

September 16

QUIET TIME NOTES:

- Expect Jesus to bring His ladder into our pit.
- Live with expectation. God desires to bless you—often in unexpected ways. Don't be so preoccupied that you miss it! Expect good.
- "Give us aid against the enemy, for human help is worthless." —Psalm 60:11
- "The way we deal with uncertainty says a lot about whether Jesus is ahead of us leading or behind us just carrying our stuff." —Bob Goff, *Live in Grace, Walk in Love*

My Takeaway:

Expect Jesus to bring His ladder into our pit.

September 17

QUIET TIME NOTES:

- Jesus lived entirely for others.

- Jesus gave up His own will to do the will of God. He proved His love for God and for us by putting our good above His own. He died to give us His Peace.

- "The fruit of…righteousness will be peace; its effect will be quietness and confidence forever." —Isaiah 32:17

- His fruit is His peace, given to us so that we can confidently trust His love. He quiets our anxious hearts. He died to give His peace to us. What have I done for someone else today to put their good above my own? Will I live my life to honor God like He did? There is no short cut. I need to trust Jesus' example.

- Help me, Lord, to overcome my disobedient, self-directed heart.

My Takeaway:

Jesus lived entirely for others.

September 18

QUIET TIME NOTES:

- My life is my time, and my time is my tithe.
- "What does the LORD your God ask of you but to fear the LORD your God, to walk in obedience to him, to love him, to serve the LORD your God with all your heart and with all your soul...Bring everything I command you...your tithes and special gifts." —Deuteronomy 10:12 & 12:11
- "Let us run with perseverance the race marked out for us." —Hebrews 12:1
- "To finish first, you must first finish." —Rick Mears, PassItOn.com
- Live like someone left the gate open!

My Takeaway:

My life is my time, and my time is my tithe. Serve God well.

September 19

QUIET TIME NOTES:

- Trust precedes peace, and peace is packaged in God's whispered Word.
- A troubled surface of a lake will not reflect an image.
- When the clatter of the world dies down, we hear the whisper of God.
- "You worship God when you choose to believe His Word over others' words." —Craig Denison, First15
- "Because he loves me," says the LORD, "I will rescue him… protect him…answer him…be with him in trouble…satisfy him and show him my salvation." —Psalm 91:14-16
- "To all who believed him and accepted him, he gave the right to become children of God." —John 1:12 NLT

My Takeaway:

Trust precedes peace, and peace is packaged in God's whispered Word.

September 20

QUIET TIME NOTES:

- God sees our faith. He also sees a fake!
- If we are righteous in our own eyes, we will fail to repent and put our trust in Jesus Christ, the only one who can save us.
- "Why do you call me, 'Lord, Lord,' and do not do what I say?" —Luke 6:46
- Is my work done out of obedience so I'm closer to Jesus, or done just to keep me occupied?

My Takeaway:

God sees our faith.
He also sees a fake!

September 21

QUIET TIME NOTES:

- We are accountable to God for living lives that bless others.

- "The only way to keep what you have is to give it away."
  —*The Word for You Today*

- "Let each one examine his own work…Do not be deceived, God is not mocked; for whatever a man sows, that he will also reap." —Galatians 6:4, 7

- "Once more a remnant…will take root below and bear fruit above." —Isaiah 37:31

My Takeaway:

We are accountable to God for living lives that bear fruit and bless others.

September 22

QUIET TIME NOTES:

- Key to grace: know who I'm living for…myself or God.
- "Make vows to the LORD your God and fulfill them."
  —Psalm 76:11
- "If the Spirit of God has stirred you, make as many of your decisions as possible irrevocable."
  —Oswald Chambers, *My Utmost for His Highest*
- We can't choose how or when we die, but we choose how we live.
- "The proof of spiritual maturity is not how 'pure' you are but awareness of your impurity. That very awareness opens the door to grace." —Philip Yancey, *What's So Amazing About Grace?*

My Takeaway:

Who am I living for: myself or God ALMIGHTY?

September 23

QUIET TIME NOTES:

- What you believe about God will show up in how you live.
- "Come near to God and he will come near to you." —James 4:8
- "See, the former things have taken place, and new things I declare." —Isaiah 42:9
- So much of our worrying is caused by trying to control things without God's direction and power. The key to rest is trusting that God is our good Father.
- "A Bible that is falling apart usually belongs to a Christian who isn't." —Charles H. Spurgeon

My Takeaway:

God widens our path when we believe Him and stop worrying.

September 24

QUIET TIME NOTES:

- When I take hold of God's hand, He will lead me out of my selfish desires.
- Don't blame the Devil for stuff you did all by yourself.
- "Think of the last thing you prayed about—
  were you devoted to your desire or to God?"
  —Oswald Chambers, *My Utmost for His Highest*
- Obey God just as you'd want your children to obey you.
- "I cling to you; your right hand upholds me." —Psalm 63:8

My Takeaway:

When I take hold of God's hand, He will lead me out of my selfish desires.

September 25

QUIET TIME NOTES:

- Prepare to trust. Trust = Rest.
- Thank you, Jesus, for your immovable rest.
- "Come to me, all you who are weary and burdened, and I will give you rest…for your souls." —Matthew 11:28-29
- "All of God's people are ordinary people who have been made extraordinary by the purpose He has given them." —Oswald Chambers, *My Utmost for His Highest*
- "Whoever trusts in the LORD is kept safe." —Proverbs 29:25
- It's inconceivable to me that God trusts me completely with free will, yet often I completely fail to trust Him.

My Takeaway:

God's purpose for me is to trust Him completely.

September 26

QUIET TIME NOTES:

- Peace is assured.
- Jesus died to give us His peace. The first thing He said to His disciples after His resurrection was: "Peace be with you!" (John 20:19.)
- Live with an assurance that you can trust His gift of peace. Peace = trust and assurance.
- "I am leaving you with a gift—peace of mind and heart. And the peace I give is a gift the world cannot give. So don't be troubled or afraid." —John 14:27 NLT
- "I have told you all this so that you may have peace in me. Here on earth, you will have many trials and sorrows. But take heart, because I have overcome the world." —John 16:33 NLT

My Takeaway:

Peace is assured.

September 27

QUIET TIME NOTES:

- Turn to God to turn on His power.
- "Days are scrolls: Write on them what you want remembered." —*Gates of Repentance*
- "The LORD *is* on my side; I will not fear. What can man do to me?" —Psalm 118:6 NKJV
- "Make the most of every opportunity in these evil days." —Ephesians 5:16 NLT
- Turning to God makes for days worth remembering.

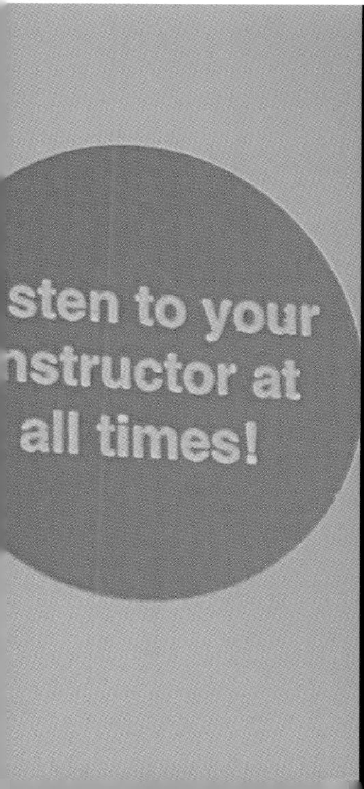

My Takeaway:

Redeem wasted time by living with an eternal perspective.

September 28

QUIET TIME NOTES:

- Fear of the LORD is the complete opposite of human fear.
- Worry prepares us for panic.
- We must break away from the world's attachments to cling to Jesus Christ.
- "Whom have you so dreaded and feared that you have not been true to me, and have neither remembered me nor taken this to heart?" —Isaiah 57:11
- "Seek the LORD while he may be found." —Isaiah 55:6

My Takeaway:

Fear of the LORD is the complete opposite of human fear.

September 29

QUIET TIME NOTES:

- God's love has no time limit.

- "You can't love in a hurry."
—Keri Wyatt Kent, *The Word for You Today*

- "Go forward into the future bravely and unafraid."
—A.J. Russell, *God Calling*

- "He who began a good work in you will carry it on to completion until the day of Christ Jesus." —Philippians 1:6

- "No, I will not abandon you as orphans—I will come to you… Since I live, you also will live." —John 14:18-19 NLT

My Takeaway:

God's love has no time limit. Trust His love to go with you always.

September 30

QUIET TIME NOTES:

- Live today with God—or your effort is wasted.
- "Jesus' primary consideration is my absolute annihilation of my right to myself and my identification with Him." —Oswald Chambers, *My Utmost for His Highest*
- "You need not fear the future, for I am already there." —Sarah Young, *Jesus Calling*
- "Instead, you ought to say, 'If it is the Lord's will, we will live and do this or that.'" —James 4:15
- "[Our] work will be shown for what it is…the fire will test the quality of each person's work." —1 Corinthians 3:13

My Takeaway:

Live today with God—or your effort is wasted.

October 1

QUIET TIME NOTES:

- Friends share the not-OK times.
- With Jesus, you don't have to pretend everything is OK.
- "What are people, that you should make so much of us, that you should think of us so often? For you examine us every morning and test us every moment." —Job 7:17-18 NLT
- Nothing is insignificant to God.
- "I will listen. If you look for me wholeheartedly, you will find me." —Jeremiah 29:12-13 NLT
- Ask Jesus to love people through you.
- "I have called you friends." —John 15:15

My Takeaway:

God knows we're not OK and still wants us close to Him to share every moment of life.

October 2

QUIET TIME NOTES:

- Obey in the ordinary moments today for an extraordinary eternity.
- All God asks is our willingness to obey!
- It is in the ordinary things in life that we prove faithful. Will we be skeptical simply because we are in the valley?
- "[God's] choicest wreaths are always wet with tears." —*Streams in the Desert*
- "A race to the finish line has a different sense of purpose and urgency than a jog around the block." —Carolyn Arends, *The Word for You Today*
- "Forgetting what is behind and straining toward what is ahead…[for] our citizenship is in Heaven." —Philippians 3:13, 20

My Takeaway:

Obey in the ordinary moments today for an extraordinary eternity.

October 3

QUIET TIME NOTES:

- In the end, I'll have to face God with how I lived my life.
- A steady commitment to excellence births opportunity.
- "It is not what a man does that determines if his work is sacred or secular, it is why he does it." —A.W. Tozer
- "Each of us will give an account of ourselves to God." —Romans 14:12 (Perhaps the most terrifying words in Scripture!)
- No more slouching through life!

My Takeaway:

In the end, I'll have to face God with how I lived my life.

October 4

QUIET TIME NOTES:

- We are transformed by forgiveness!
- We are formed, reformed, and transformed by God's love.
- "The Father…has qualified you to share in the inheritance of his holy people in the kingdom of light. For he has rescued us from the dominion of darkness." —Colossians 1:12-13
- "Before you were born I set you apart." —Jeremiah 1:5
- We are powerless without God's power.

My Takeaway:

We are formed, reformed, and transformed. We are rescued, redeemed, and forgiven. We are transformed by forgiveness!

October 5

QUIET TIME NOTES:

- Jesus alone gives us hope.
- I "read my pardon in the wounds of Jesus."
  —Arthur G. Bennett, *The Valley of Vision*
- "Earth has no sorrow that heaven can't heal." —Thomas Moore
- Jesus died to deliver us from sin. Would I refuse Him?
- "Light has come into the world, but people loved darkness instead of light because their deeds were evil." —John 3:19
- Prayer splits heaven open.

My Takeaway:

Jesus alone holds heaven open to us. He is our only hope.

October 6

QUIET TIME NOTES:

- Jesus came to earth to forgive me in person.
- We don't have to live in condemnation when we mess up. Even Paul said, "For I do not do the good I want to do, but the evil I do not want to do—this I keep on doing" (Romans 7:19).
- "When you were dead in your sins…God made you alive with Christ. He forgave us all our sins…nailing [them] to the cross." —Colossians 2:13-14

My Takeaway:

God knows I mess up, so He came to earth to forgive me in person.

October 7

QUIET TIME NOTES:

- We let our insecurities direct our lives while God is looking for ordinary people to do extraordinary things that *He* directs.
- The move from self-power to God's power comes when we realize we are powerless.
- "Why has the land been ruined?...It is because they have forsaken my law...they have not obeyed me or followed my law." —Jeremiah 9:12-13
- "And whatever you do, whether in word or deed, do it all in the name of the Lord Jesus, giving thanks..." —Colossians 3:17

My Takeaway:

God provides power when we pay attention to Him.

October 8

QUIET TIME NOTES:

- God restores peace in the midst of our suffering when we stop striving. Easy to say, hard to do.

- "After you have suffered a little while, [God] will himself restore you and make you strong, firm and steadfast." —1 Peter 5:10

- "Whatever you do…do it all in the name of the Lord." —Colossians 3:17

- "Peace your inmost soul will fill/ When you're still!" —*Streams in the Desert*

My Takeaway:

God restores peace in the midst of our suffering when we stop striving.

October 9

QUIET TIME NOTES:

- May I guard my minutes to be useful for God's concerns.
- If you know the thief is coming, lock the door! Lord Jesus, guard the door of my heart from the enemy. Help me to quickly identify and resist his attacks.
- "Learn to know the present value of single minutes and endeavor to let not one particle fall useless to the ground." —Samuel Johnson
- "Seek the LORD while he may be found." —Isaiah 55:6

My Takeaway:

My time can be a blessing to others, or I can use it for self-indulgence.

October 10

QUIET TIME NOTES:

- When Jesus saves us from our self-erected barricades, we soften—and are able to forgive and extend grace to others.
- If I wallow in self-pity, I create my own world and block goodness from melting my frozen heart.
- God often steps in to save us at the point we least expect it.
- "Sometimes we are in such a hurry to 'fix' people we don't have time to sympathize with them." —*The Word for You Today*
- "Bear with each other and forgive one another if any of you has a grievance against someone. Forgive as the Lord forgave you." —Colossians 3:13

My Takeaway:

When Jesus saves us from our self-erected barricades, we melt—and are able to forgive and extend grace to others.

October 11

QUIET TIME NOTES:

- Silence is deep trust.
- I hurt myself when I listen to myself.
- God's silence can be a blessing—the silence of intimacy with a daughter or son He trusts. (Ever notice how you never have an awkward silence around someone you love deeply?)
- "The only thing you absolutely need is the one thing you can never lose: My Presence with you." —Sarah Young, *Jesus Calling*
- "You are a chosen people…that you may declare the praises of him who called you out of darkness into his wonderful light." —1 Peter 2:9

My Takeaway:

Silence isn't dark abandonment—it's genuine trust.

October 12

QUIET TIME NOTES:

- God uses our ordinary days to renovate our character.
- The true test of integrity takes place in everyday moments when no one is looking.
- "Renewal" means that you've been renovated from the inside out.
- "He who began a good work in you will carry it on to completion." —Philippians 1:6
- "The one who calls you is faithful, and he will do it." —1 Thessalonians 5:24

My Takeaway:

God uses our ordinary days to renovate our character.

October 13

QUIET TIME NOTES:

- Calm down and claim Christ's peace. It lasts forever. Today doesn't.
- "May I never think I prosper unless my soul prospers...May I value things in relation to eternity." —Arthur G. Bennett, *The Valley of Vision*
- "Do not be anxious about anything, but in every situation, by prayer and petition, with thanksgiving, present your requests to God. And the peace of God... will guard your hearts and your minds in Christ Jesus." —Philippians 4:6-7

My Takeaway:

Calm down and claim Christ's peace. It lasts forever. Today doesn't.

October 14

QUIET TIME NOTES:

- The unknown is known to God.
- "Oh, that their hearts would be inclined to fear me and keep all my commands always, so that it might go well with them and their children forever!" —Deuteronomy 5:29
- We can ask great things of a great God.
- Let God direct your day even when it seems like chaos is swirling around you.
- "Whatever you think about the most grows…The more you think about something, the stronger it grows in your brain." —Dr. Caroline Leaf, *Switch on Your Brain Every Day*†
- "A man reaps what he sows." —Galatians 6:7

† Dr. Carolyn Leaf, *Switch on Your Brain Every Day*, 2018, Baker Publishing Group.

My Takeaway:

The unknown is known to God—so let God grow in you.

October 15

QUIET TIME NOTES:

- "Be blessed with knowing your Father is there for you at all times…Be blessed in the name of Jehovah-Shammah, the Lord who promises to be present with you always." —Sylvia Gunter
- "Pray that we may be delivered from wicked and evil people, for not everyone has faith." —2 Thessalonians 3:2
- "Show us your unfailing love, LORD, and grant us your salvation." —Psalm 85:7
- God won't fight to get our attention.

My Takeaway:

God is merciful when we pay more attention to Him than our pain.

October 16

QUIET TIME NOTES:

- Worship unlocks God's unfailing love.
- The Church is God's hospital for whatever ails us and causes pain.
- "In his unfailing love, my God will stand with me." —Psalm 59:10 NLT
- "For the Spirit God gave us does not make us timid, but gives us power, love and self-discipline." —2 Timothy 1:7

My Takeaway:

Worshiping with others in church heals us, strengthens our spirit, and cleanses our minds. Praise unlocks God's unfailing love.

October 17

QUIET TIME NOTES:

- Believe you are being heard. Our heavenly WiFi hotspot is the cross.

- We say we've surrendered, but we keep believing in ourselves. Yet Christ takes our words at face value and gives us His cross. It might be difficult to carry at times, but we will exchange it for a crown if we continue to believe He is our Savior.

- "Lord, save us from ourselves." —Mario Zandstra

- When you pray, trust that God heard you and will answer with whatever is best for you.

- "But when you ask, you must believe and not doubt, because the one who doubts is like a wave of the sea… That person should not expect to receive anything from the Lord." —James 1:6-7

My Takeaway:

Believe you are being heard, then relax. He's got this.

October 18

QUIET TIME NOTES:

- True love for God doesn't falter when I'm falling apart.
- "Sir," Gideon replied, "if the LORD is with us, why has all this happened to us?" —Judges 6:13 NLT
- Do I love God or do I only love His blessings?
- "Do you seek great things for yourself?" —Jeremiah 45:5 (This verse has a greater context but still asks this question.)
- We worship so we don't forget God's splendor and think we can do it all ourselves.

My Takeaway:

True love for God doesn't falter when I'm falling apart.

October 19

QUIET TIME NOTES:

- God promises to pardon and provide when we repent.
- "Your eyes are open to the ways of all mankind." —Jeremiah 32:19
- "I will cleanse them from all the sin they have committed against me and will forgive…" —Jeremiah 33:8
- "I will make an everlasting covenant with them: I will never stop doing good to them, and I will inspire them to fear me, so that they will never turn away from me." —Jeremiah 32:40
- "This is what the LORD says: As I have brought all this great calamity on this people, so I will give them all the prosperity I have promised them." —Jeremiah 32:42

My Takeaway:

God promises to pardon. He sees us and yet provides a way out of our messy sin.

October 20

QUIET TIME NOTES:

- I have to empty my heart of myself if I want God to fill me.
- If God doesn't fill me with His Spirit, it's because I'm full of myself…I've not surrendered.
- You can't look at yourself and God at the same time.
- Don't search the Bible looking for a rationalization for your actions. Search for God.
- "Throw off your old sinful nature and your former way of life…Instead…put on your new nature, created to be like God—truly righteous and holy." —Ephesians 4:22-24 NLT

My Takeaway:

I have to empty my heart of myself if I want God to fill me.

October 21

QUIET TIME NOTES:

- What if we took God at His word? We'd know we are His!
- "Sometimes we have to let go of our plans to take hold of God's purpose." —Sharon Jaynes
- "Most of our worries can be summed up in two words: 'What if?'" —*The Word for You Today*
- "The LORD himself goes before you and will be with you; he will never leave you nor forsake you. Do not be afraid; do not be discouraged." —Deuteronomy 31:8

My Takeaway:

What if we took God at his word? We'd know we are His! (He tells us so!)

October 22

QUIET TIME NOTES:

- Only repentance opens our spirit to radiate God.

- "Simply knowing right and wrong doesn't make someone righteous; only repentance leads someone to righteousness, and ultimately to salvation through Jesus Christ."
—Robert Wiese, *Lessons of the Coming Kingdom: Thy Kingdom come. Thy will be done.*

- "Moses only reflected the glory of God; the dedicated believer radiates the glory of God."
—Warren Wiersbe, *Be Delivered*

- "Do you not know that you are the temple of God and that the Spirit of God dwells in you?" —1 Corinthians 3:16 NKJV

My Takeaway:

Only repentance opens our spirit to radiate God.

October 23

QUIET TIME NOTES:

- Enjoyment comes as we share God's gifts.
- "Command those who are rich in this present world not to be arrogant nor to put their hope in wealth, which is so uncertain, but to put their hope in God, who richly provides us with everything for our enjoyment. Command them to do good, to be rich in good deeds, and to be generous and willing to share." —1 Timothy 6:17-18
- "And I am praying that you will put into action the generosity that comes from your faith as you understand and experience all the good things we have in Christ." —Philemon 6 NLT

My Takeaway:

I'm humbled by the beautiful home God has entrusted to us. May we share it well—with welcome and worship.

October 24

QUIET TIME NOTES:

- Praise can be perilously packed around pain.
- God never gives a trial without intending a compassionate blessing.
- "It is through pain that God gets the most out of us... The sharper the Craftsman's knives, the finer and more beautiful his work." — *Streams in the Desert*
- "But mark this: There will be terrible times in the last days. People will be lovers of themselves...rather than lovers of God." —2 Timothy 3:1-2, 4

My Takeaway:

Praise can be perilously packed around pain.

October 25

QUIET TIME NOTES:

- Why do we trust God with our eternity but not our earthly endeavors?

- Don't give your leftovers to God—give your first fruits. Leftovers are tied to self-sufficiency while first-fruit giving is God's sufficiency. —*The Word for You Today*, my paraphrase

- "Even now," declares the LORD, "return to me with all your heart, with fasting and weeping and mourning. Rend your heart and not your garments. Return to the LORD your God, for he is gracious and compassionate, slow to anger and abounding in love, and he relents from sending calamity. Who knows? He may turn and relent and leave behind a blessing." —Joel 2:12-14

My Takeaway:

Why do we trust God with our eternity but not our earthly endeavors?

October 26

QUIET TIME NOTES:

- What is God's will? "Rejoice always, pray continually, give thanks in all circumstances; for this is God's will for you in Christ Jesus." —1 Thessalonians 5:16-18

- Rejoice, pray, give thanks. Notice the proportions—it's three parts.

- Meet with Jesus alone. Spend time with God alone. He wants you to Himself.

- "He went up on a mountainside by himself to pray… He was there alone." —Matthew 14:23

My Takeaway:

To live a life of continual prayer, rejoice always and always be thankful.

October 27

QUIET TIME NOTES:

- God sees our lives cluttered—and offers calm.
- Our lives become cluttered by abundance. So pack light as you travel through this life.
- "We don't like to wait for anything, including God...While we are waiting, God is working. The sign on God's waiting room reads, 'Be still, and know that I am God' (Psalm 46:10)." —*The Word for You Today*
- We might not like it, but patience is only developed through problems.
- "You are not willing to come to Me that you may have life." —John 5:40 NKJV

My Takeaway:

God sees our lives cluttered with impatience—yet to those who believe Him, He offers eternal calm.

October 28

QUIET TIME NOTES:

- Enjoy life by loving with energy and excellence.

- Go, eat your bread with joy, and drink your wine with a merry heart. (Enjoy life.)

  Let your garments always be white. (Be pure, stay with God.)

  And let your head lack no oil. (Care for yourself.)

  Live joyfully with the wife whom you love. (Share life with family.) —Based on Ecclesiastes 9:7-9 NKJV

- "Whatever your hand finds to do, do it with your might; for there is no work or device or knowledge or wisdom in the grave where you are going." —Ecclesiastes 9:10 NKJV

My Takeaway:

God encourages us to work hard but enjoy life, taking care of both family and self. Enjoy life by loving with energy and excellence.

October 29

QUIET TIME NOTES:

- Prayer unsticks us from earth.
- God customizes our thorns. He is more interested in our character than our comfort. Ouch!
- God had limitless compassion in allowing His Son to suffer and die.
- In prayer I enter the *eternal* world.
- "God's love has been poured out into our hearts through the Holy Spirit." —Romans 5:5
- "It is finished." —John 19:30

My Takeaway:

God's gift of life through His love dissolves what glues us to earth. Prayer unsticks us.

October 30

QUIET TIME NOTES:

- "And He wanted the finest gold/ To mold as a crown for the King to wear."
  —Arthur Tappan Pierson, *Streams in the Desert*

- "I went past the field of a sluggard…and learned a lesson from what I saw." —Proverbs 24:30, 32

- "Slothful men never take the trouble to think.
  Am I using the minutes as they fly?
  We each have some power to serve God.
  Do you plan to neglect God until the end of your existence?
  Am I storing up thorns for my dying pillow?
  We cannot live in this world as entire blanks; we shall either do good or do evil, as sure as we are alive."
  —Charles H. Spurgeon, *Talks to Farmers*

My Takeaway:

The way we live determines what we will have to give to God.

October 31

QUIET TIME NOTES:

- When we turn our sobbing spirit to Jesus, He talks to God for us.
- "Restore us to yourself, LORD, that we may return; renew our days as of old." —Lamentations 5:21
- "How shall we escape if we ignore so great a salvation?" —Hebrews 2:3
- "How sweet it is to fall into the embrace of His blessed arms and to simply sob out the sorrow that we cannot speak!" —*Streams in the Desert*
- "We do not know what we ought to pray for, but the Spirit himself intercedes for us…" —Romans 8:26

My Takeaway:

When we turn our sobbing spirit to Jesus, He talks to God for us.

November 1

QUIET TIME NOTES:

- May my actions never block someone's view of God's light.
- "Arise, shine; for your light has come! And the glory of the LORD is risen upon you." —Isaiah 60:1 NKJV
- "In humility value others above yourselves, not looking to your own interests but each of you to the interests of the others." —Philippians 2:3-4
- I will strive to conduct myself now in a way that will enhance my witness for Christ—even after a contentious election. (My reflection after reading a post by Dr. Jim Denison.)

My Takeaway:

May my actions never block someone's view of God's light.

November 2

QUIET TIME NOTES:

- Lukewarm complacency ignores what Christ gave for us.
- "We make a living by what we get, a life by what we give." —Winston Churchill
- "Complacency is a deadly foe of all spiritual growth…[Christ] waits to be wanted!" —A.W. Tozer, quoted by Dr. Jim Denison
- "Neglect is all that is needed to produce evil…The heart cannot be altogether empty; either Christ or the devil will possess it…Probably the worst people in the world are those who have the best intentions but never carry them out. In that way Satan lulls many to sleep." —Charles H. Spurgeon, *Talks to Farmers*

My Takeaway:

Neglecting what Christ gave us is at the core of complacency—and one of Satan's strongest techniques.

November 3

QUIET TIME NOTES:

- "…May [the peoples] call on the name of the LORD, to serve Him with one accord." —Zephaniah 3:9 NKJV
- "Love your enemies, do good to those who hate you, bless those who curse you, pray for those who mistreat you." —Luke 6:27-28
- "Picking a fight is easy. Loving each other when we disagree is how we grow." —Bob Goff, *Live in Grace, Walk in Love*
- God doesn't force us to obey.
- "Sweet land of liberty, let freedom ring." —"America the Beautiful," 1893

My Takeaway:

It takes all of us obeying the Golden Rule to keep America free.

November 4

QUIET TIME NOTES:

- We can't fake love. God knows our hearts.
- "Relationships have the power to transform us in ways opinions never will." —Bob Goff, *Live in Grace, Walk in Love*
- "When you ask, you do not receive, because you ask with wrong motives, that you may spend what you get on your pleasures." —James 4:3
- You won't find the words I, me, my, or mine in the Lord's Prayer. But you do find "give *us*," "forgive *us*," and "deliver *us*." God knows what you want and why you want it. —*The Word for You Today*, my paraphrase

My Takeaway:

Our relationship with God centers on truly loving others more than self. We can't fake it. He knows our hearts.

November 5

QUIET TIME NOTES:

- Prayer opens heaven.
- "Grant me more and more to prize the privilege of prayer." —Arthur G. Bennett, *The Valley of Vision*
- "I do not delay My second coming. My followers delay it. If each lived for Me, by Me, in Me…then long ago the world would have been drawn to Me."—A.J. Russell, *God Calling*
- Oh Lord, the truth cuts deep.
- "I am with you and will watch over you wherever you go, and I will bring you back to this land." —Genesis 28:15 (As I read this today, I think of "this land" as heaven.)

My Takeaway:

Prayer takes us to heaven.

November 6

QUIET TIME NOTES:

- God knows who we put first in our lives.
- "You can't pray, 'Lord, what do you want me to do?' when you already know what to do but aren't willing to do it. If you're serious about getting your prayers answered, read the fine print!" —*The Word for You Today*
- To believe is to commit. Am I committed to Jesus or to myself?
- "Love is patient, love is kind." —1 Corinthians 13:4
- "If eternity is all the time ever, we're already a part of eternity…Let's start treating each other like we'll be together for eternity." —Bob Goff, *Live in Grace, Walk in Love*

My Takeaway:

God is pretty clear on this: You can love others when you love Jesus more than yourself. God knows who is first in our lives.

November 7

QUIET TIME NOTES:

- It's hard to write with tears. Peace comes from Christ alone.
- "Sing to the LORD, for he has done glorious things." —Isaiah 12:5
- "He...will rejoice over you with singing." —Zephaniah 3:17
- "The light of life is a finite flame...Like a candle, the flames dance, and our life is full. But as night follows day, the candle of our life burns down and gutters. There is an end to the flames...Yet we do not despair, for we are more than a memory slowly fading into darkness. With our lives, we give life. Something of us can never die: We move in the eternal cycle of darkness and death, of light and life...May the source of peace send peace to all who mourn." —*Gates of Repentance*
- I praise God for life. My good friend Susan went to heaven last night. I loved her and am in tears, but this morning God has graciously given me joy for her life.

My Takeaway:

Peace comes from faith in Christ alone.

November 8

QUIET TIME NOTES:

- Obeying God is cooperation that can transform us.
- "Partial obedience is actually disobedience."
—Dr. Charles Stanley
- When I receive blessings from God, may I not forget that the greatest dangers arise from my benefits.
- We can either complain to God or cooperate.
- "Do not conform to the pattern of this world, but be transformed by the renewing of your mind." —Romans 12:2
- "Though it linger, wait for it." —Habakkuk 2:3

My Takeaway:

Obeying God is cooperation that can transform us.

November 9

QUIET TIME NOTES:

- Fix what's broken in your life while you still can.
- "Thorns had come up everywhere...and the stone wall was in ruins." —Proverbs 24:31
- "Broken fences remove the boundary so the protection is gone. Good things go out and bad things come in." —Charles H. Spurgeon, *Talks to Farmers*
- Would you be ready if Jesus showed up today?

My Takeaway:

Fix what's broken in your life while you still can.

November 10

QUIET TIME NOTES:

- Time is our opportunity to be kind before we run out of it.
- Extreme conditions create opportunities to adapt. Nothing on earth stays the same; change is inevitable.
- Our time gives us opportunities to know God's love.
- Be remembered for small kindnesses more than great achievements.
- "Who can praise you from the grave?" —Psalm 6:5, NLT

My Takeaway:

Extreme kindness transcends time.

November 11

QUIET TIME NOTES:

- Yesterday was our move-in day. After greeting us, the driver decided to turn the truck around so he could back into our driveway, but the steep slope of the hill caught the tailgate and wedged the truck against the hill. It was very stuck.

  I stood there and prayed for God to send one of his huge, mighty angels to lift the truck just a bit to free it. Nothing happened at first, but then a garbage truck came down the road. They stopped to help. After an hour, they had to go finish their rounds, but they returned later and pulled the truck to freedom with a tow belt from the auto parts store. I told Matthew, the garbage truck driver, that I had prayed for angelic help, and he was that for us yesterday!

My Takeaway:

God does hear and answer in the most unexpected ways. For us, it was the trash guys.

November 12

QUIET TIME NOTES:

- You can have good intentions, but gratitude alone moves us to act in love toward others.
- "It is easy for the painful things of this year to drown out the many things we have to be thankful for." (Written during the first year of COVID-19.) —Sylvia Gunter
- "Love your neighbor as yourself…Do this and you will live." —Luke 10:27-28
- "Obedience begins with knowing what to do, but we haven't been obedient until it is done." —Janet Denison

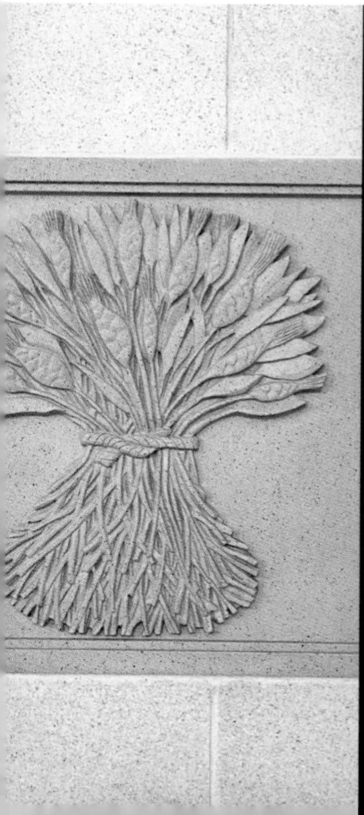

My Takeaway:

You can have good intentions, but gratitude alone moves us to act in love toward others.

November 13

QUIET TIME NOTES:

- Christ's forgiveness is freedom not probation.
- "When faith sleeps, my heart becomes an unclean thing…the cage of unclean lusts all fluttering to escape." —Arthur G. Bennett, *The Valley of Vision*
- "May the God of hope fill you with all joy and peace as you trust in him, so that you may overflow with hope by the power of the Holy Spirit." —Romans 15:13
- "Unconfessed, unforgiven sin will make you miserable." —*The Word for You Today*
- Conviction + Confession = Cleansing + Confidence
- "First we make our choices. Then our choices make us." —Anne Frank

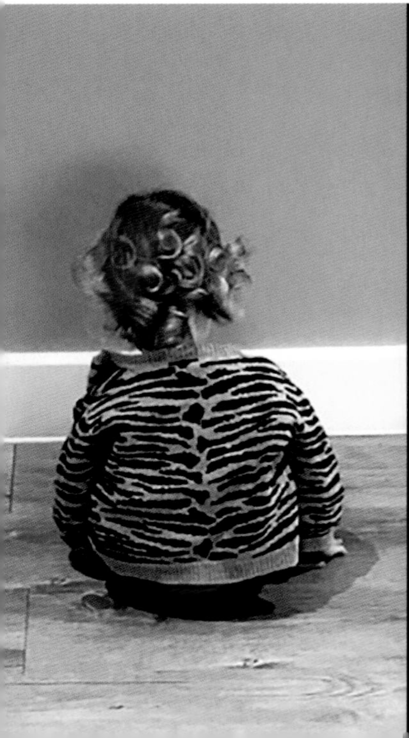

My Takeaway:

Faith in Christ alone is our confidence in the confessions we make. Confession remakes who you are.

November 14

QUIET TIME NOTES:

- Between unpacking and moving I've been very distracted, and I've missed my quiet time more than I'd like. So this morning, I felt I needed to sit down and read Psalm 16. I'm so blessed that God met me exactly where I am today, and I'm feeling grateful to have home and family!

  But I'm even more blessed because of His promise: "The boundary lines have fallen for me in pleasant places; surely I have a delightful inheritance...I keep my eyes always on the LORD. With him at my right hand, I will not be shaken" (Psalm 16:6, 8). This promise is for you too!

My Takeaway:

The boundary lines have fallen for me in pleasant places—I believe!

November 15

QUIET TIME NOTES:

- Trials turn our attention to God and away from all our other gods.

- Nothing but great trials can teach us to trust God's promises.

- "No one ever feels better the week after they enter recovery…The pain might be a sign of progress." —Bob Goff, *Live in Grace, Walk in Love*

- "To pray is not to sit there and fantasize and daydream. To pray is to look at Jesus who is real and to believe more and more." —Henri J. Nouwen, *You Are the Beloved*

- "They have followed other gods…Therefore this is what the LORD says: 'I will bring on them a disaster they cannot escape.'" —Jeremiah 11:10-11

My Takeaway:

Perhaps God gives us trials to get our attention and to make a way to bring us back to Him.

November 16

QUIET TIME NOTES:

- God rewards His champions. Don't give up.
- "The best things are always achieved by the most difficult paths…for the express purpose of enabling you to win your crown." —*Streams in the Desert*
- "Prize fighter James Corbett was once asked, 'What's the most important thing for a man to do to become a champion?' He replied, 'Fight one more round.'" —*The Word for You Today*
- "The Lord God will help me." —Isaiah 50:7 NKJV

My Takeaway:

God will help us
if we don't give up
on Him.

November 17

QUIET TIME NOTES:

- You can't cheat God into blessing you.
- "The same wind that blew at your back on your way to hell will blow in your face on your way to heaven." —*The Word for You Today*
- "Oh…that you would not light useless fires on my altar!… Cursed is the cheat." —Malachi 1:10, 14
- "'Return to me, and I will return to you,' says the LORD Almighty." —Malachi 3:7

My Takeaway:

You can't cheat God into blessing you. You have to return to Him and obey His rules.

November 18

QUIET TIME NOTES:

- He gives me the tools to make me who He wants me to be.

- Jesus can't be my redeemer if I'm my own savior. Faith accepts him as Redeemer and LORD, or not at all.
  —Arthur Bennett, *Valley of Vision*, my paraphrase

- "Strive to be the friend I see in My vision of you."
  —A.J. Russell, *God Calling*

- "The gifts of the Spirit are not toys to play with. They are tools to build with and weapons to fight with." —Greg Laurie

My Takeaway:

God remakes me with his tools—to be the person He envisioned me to be. To be His friend!

November 19

QUIET TIME NOTES:

- Triumph over our struggles requires dependence on God.
- "Struggle for a better world not out of frustration, resentment, anger or self-righteousness, but out of care, love, forgiveness, and gratitude." —Henri J. Nouwen
- "Even the longest day has a sunset." —*Streams in the Desert*
- "Though you have made me see troubles, many and bitter, you will restore my life again." —Psalm 71:20
- "God expects nothing from you but failure!...But He has given the Holy Spirit to you so that you need not fail." —*The Word for You Today*
- "He who abides in Me, and I in him, bears much fruit; for without Me you can do nothing." —John 15:5

My Takeaway:

Triumph over our struggles requires dependence on God.

November 20

QUIET TIME NOTES:

- Isolating ourselves from God makes us vulnerable to attack.
- "Storms in our lives reveal what we really believe about Jesus. And when you know that God is always with you, no matter what you face you can make it." —Greg Laurie
- Isolation has a way of weakening us. When we feel as if we are the only ones struggling in life, we become vulnerable to the spiritual attacks of the devil. Our enemy wants to disconnect us from each other as a lion cuts off prey from the herd.
- "Be alert and of sober mind. Your enemy the devil prowls around like a roaring lion looking for someone to devour." —1 Peter 5:8

My Takeaway:

Isolating ourselves from God makes us vulnerable to attack.

November 21

QUIET TIME NOTES:

- Our plans are useless unless we allow God to use us during impossible times. I think God chuckles at what we think is impossible.

- "Length of days does not profit me except the days are passed in thy presence, in thy service, to thy glory." —Arthur G. Bennett, *The Valley of Vision*

- "No matter how close to the edge of the cliff He may lead you, never snatch the guiding reins from His hands." —*Streams in the Desert*

- "Is anything too hard for me?" —Jeremiah 32:27

- "Blessed is the one who waits." —Daniel 12:12

My Takeaway:

Our plans are useless unless we allow God to use us during impossible times

November 22

QUIET TIME NOTES:

- True victory comes only through trusting Christ.
- God holds all of our affairs in His hands. But often we are clinging so desperately to one particular blessing that we can't receive all that He has for us.
- "Outrunning your rival doesn't mean you ran your best race." —Richard C. Halverson, *The Word for You Today*
- Don't congratulate yourself thinking "I'm safe" when you follow the desires of your own stubborn heart. —Deuteronomy 29:19, my paraphrase
- "They forgot…the wonders he had shown them…They did not believe in God or trust in his deliverance." —Psalm 78:11, 22

My Takeaway:

My race is against my own stubborn heart, and true victory comes only through trusting Christ.

November 23

QUIET TIME NOTES:

- Perhaps God gives us wisdom and blessings when we intercede for others.

- "God never gives us discernment so that we may criticize, but that we may intercede." —Oswald Chambers, *My Utmost for His Highest*

- "Give me understanding, so that I may keep your law and obey it with all my heart." —Psalm 119:34

- "Blessed are those who find wisdom, those who gain understanding." —Proverbs 3:13

- "Hell begins on the day God grants us a clear vision of all we might have achieved…the gifts we have wasted…all we might have done but didn't do." —Gian Carlo Menotti, *The Word for You Today*

My Takeaway:

God gives us wisdom and blessings when we intercede for others.

November 24

QUIET TIME NOTES:

- Good things come out of quiet communion with God.
- "In quietness and trust is your strength." —Isaiah 30:15
- Most of us want things to get better without having to change anything.
- "If you're on the wrong train, don't keep going—get off at the next station!" —*The Word for You Today*
- For hearts that will stop focusing on themselves, there is the "peace of God which transcends all understanding" (Philippians 4:7).

My Takeaway:

Good things come out of quiet communion with God. Stop and listen to what God is telling you.

November 25

QUIET TIME NOTES:

- Showing love today blesses our tomorrow.
- "Be sympathetic, love one another, be compassionate and humble. Do not repay evil with evil…On the contrary, repay evil with blessing…so that you may inherit a blessing…Seek peace and pursue it." —1 Peter 3:8-9, 11
- "Trust in God's future empowers us to serve God in the present." —Dr. Jim Denison

My Takeaway:

Showing love today blesses our tomorrow.

November 26

QUIET TIME NOTES:

- God is patient as we dehydrate, but when we realize that repentance matters, He will fill us with living water. Hallelujah!
- "These people are springs without water..." —2 Peter 2:17
- "Give me discernment that I may understand your statutes." —Psalm 119:125
- "The Lord is not slow...Instead he is patient with you, not wanting anyone to perish, but everyone to come to repentance." —2 Peter 3:9

My Takeaway:

God is patient as we dehydrate, but when we realize that repentance matters, He fills us with living water for true life.

November 27

QUIET TIME NOTES:

- Christ dwells in us—even as we rush. No distractions block His love.

- This morning I asked myself, "How do I dwell in the shadow of the Most High when I'm racing to get stuff done?"

- Pray for eyes that can see the beauty of God's love—because the world distorts all that we would desire.

- "I want no will laid grudgingly upon My Altar…I am answering their prayers in the best and quickest way." —A.J. Russell, *God Calling*

- "Pray that out of his glorious riches he may strengthen you with power through his Spirit in your inner being, so that Christ may dwell in your hearts through faith." —Ephesians 3:16-17

My Takeaway:

When my counter is cluttered with distractions, God's altar is not.

November 28

QUIET TIME NOTES:

- As my dog completely trusts me, I am to completely trust God.
- Our dog has no idea what today holds for him, but we know he is going to Nashville today—for a month-long stay with my daughter!
- God engineers everything and wants us to trust Him with everything.
- Our self-will is exactly what we need to nail to our personal cross—so we can get out of the way and worship Jesus.
- "If by the Spirit you put to death the misdeeds of the body, you will live." —Romans 8:13

My Takeaway:

As my dog completely trusts me, I am to trust God completely.

November 29

QUIET TIME NOTES:

- We are not pre-programmed robots. God puts free choice in us, but it still takes discipline to live well.

- “One half of knowing what you want is knowing what you must give up before you get it.”
  —American playwright Sidney Howard, *The Word for You Today*

- “Talent without discipline is like an octopus on roller skates.”
  —H. Jackson Brown, Jr.

- “From the one who has been entrusted with much, much more will be asked.” —Luke 12:48

- “God has given us the intellect…to be co-creators. As such, you have a say in the possible outcomes of your life.”
  —Dr. Carolyn Leaf, *Switch on Your Brain Every Day* †

† Dr. Carolyn Leaf, *Switch on Your Brain Every Day*, 2018, Baker Publishing Group.

My Takeaway:

We are not pre-programmed robots. God puts free choice in us, but it still takes discipline to live well.

November 30

QUIET TIME NOTES:

- Fear blocks peace.

- So easily we become troubled inside and gripped with fear! Jesus knew this would happen, and that is why His most frequent command is "Be not afraid!"

  Yet we are not to stay in this place of fear, even though it is a normal human response. God continually reminds us that He is with us, that He will take us by the hand, that He will lead us even through the valley of death.

- "Perfect love drives out fear." —1 John 4:18

My Takeaway:

Jesus came to take our fear and to give Peace on earth as it is in heaven.

December 1

QUIET TIME NOTES:

- Love here = Life there
- "Convince me that I can have no peace at death, nor hope that I should go to Christ, unless I intend to do his will and have his fullness while I live."
  —Arthur G. Bennett, *The Valley of Vision*
- "Divine Sympathy includes responsibility… Wherever your sympathy goes, you must go, too."
  —A.J. Russell, *God Calling*
- We cannot obey ourselves into heaven: We must follow Christ from a motive of love.
- "Modern man has lost the perspective of eternity."
  —Sarah Young, *Jesus Calling*
- "Because of the LORD'S great love we are not consumed."
  —Lamentations 3:22

My Takeaway:

Loving service *here* serves us well *there*.

December 2

QUIET TIME NOTES:

- Live in the True Light, not twinkle lights.
- "Arise, shine; for your light has come!" —Isaiah 60:1
- Your light reveals to the world that you've been with your Savior.
- "We tend to rely on our own energy, instead of being energized by the power that comes from identification with Jesus." —Oswald Chambers, *My Utmost for His Highest*
- "Sing and make music from your heart to the Lord." —Ephesians 5:19

My Takeaway:

As Christmas approaches, try to live in the True Light. The lights and carols are worship—not decorations.

December 3

QUIET TIME NOTES:

- Love should be simple, but we are stubborn.
- "In our culture, God is not a king but a hobby…If you want to get along with God, stay off his throne." —Dr. Jim Denison
- We see Jesus as one of us rather than KING of us.
- "The one who keeps God's commands lives in him, and he in them." —1 John 3:24
- "Let us not love with words or speech but with actions and in truth." —1 John 3:18
- "Whoever remains stiff-necked after many rebukes will suddenly be destroyed—without remedy." —Proverb 29:1

My Takeaway:

Listen up: God commands us to act o His love in us. It shou be simple, but we are stubborn, unrightfully claiming His throne.

December 4

QUIET TIME NOTES:

- Focusing on your troubles creates the trouble you fear.
- "You'll always have bad times, but they wake you up to all the good you were ignoring." —Daily Briefing, Fellowship of Christian Firefighters International
- Your thought life turns on or off epigenetic marks and signals, and makes what you think about real. —Dr. Caroline Leaf, *Switch on Your Brain Every Day,*† my paraphrase
- "Do not let your hearts be troubled and do not be afraid." —John 14:27
- "He who is in you is greater than he who is in the world." —1 John 4:4 NKJV

† Dr. Carolyn Leaf, *Switch on Your Brain Every Day*, 2018, Baker Publishing Group.

My Takeaway:

Focusing on your troubles creates the trouble you fear.

December 5

QUIET TIME NOTES:

- God gives us a cross before He gives a crown.
- Give to all whose lives you touch. First give prayer, time, yourself, love, thought…then give of this world's goods and money. —A.J. Russell, *God Calling*, my paraphrase
- I am responsible for using what God has given me—especially the temple of the Holy Spirit, including my mind, and all of my thoughts and desires.
- "Do you not know that your bodies are temples of the Holy Spirit, who is in you?" —1 Corinthians 6:19
- I am responsible for the Holy Spirit's home—oh, how I need to clean house!
- Immanuel = God with us

My Takeaway:

Giving of myself cleans the temple.

December 6

QUIET TIME NOTES:

- Eternal life is an intimate relationship with God. Christmas is the open door.

- "Eternal life is knowing God intimately—not just knowing about God, knowing of God, or knowing others who know God, but truly knowing him yourself." —Craig Denison, First15

- "Now this is eternal life: that they know you, the only true God, and Jesus Christ, whom you have sent." —John 17:3

- You may know all *about* a certain celebrity, but if you knocked on his door, he wouldn't let you in.

My Takeaway:

Christmas is an open door to intimacy with Christ

December 7

QUIET TIME NOTES:

- God's goodness is unlimited—and necessary.
- "God dispenses his goodness not with an eyedropper but with a fire hydrant." —*The Word for You Today*
- "Those who sow with tears will reap with songs of joy." —Psalm 126:5
- "Come, let us return to the LORD. He has torn us to pieces but he will heal us." —Hosea 6:1

My Takeaway:

God's goodness is unlimited—and necessary.

December 8

QUIET TIME NOTES:

- Eternal life is a gift, but it cost God His Son.
- "We trample the blood of the Son of God underfoot if we think we are forgiven because we are sorry for our sins...Our Lord does not pretend we are all right when we are all wrong." —Oswald Chambers, *My Utmost for His Highest*
- "There is no other name...by which we must be saved." —Acts 4:12
- "I am the LORD your God...there is no savior besides Me." —Hosea 13:4 NKJV
- "Break up your fallow ground, for it is time to seek the LORD." —Hosea 10:12 NKJV
- "These people are...shepherds who feed only themselves. They are clouds without rain, blown along by the wind...twice dead." —Jude 12

My Takeaway:

Don't sugarcoat your salvation; eternal life is a gift, but it cost God His Son.

December 9

QUIET TIME NOTES:

- Be kind to God's kids, especially Jesus.
- The sincerity of my faith corresponds to my fear of offending God.
- "In humility value others above yourselves...looking...to the interests of the others." —Philippians 2:3-4
- "Be kind and compassionate to one another" (Ephesians 4:32). This can and should include being kind to Jesus! I've never thought of it this way before—wow.

My Takeaway:

Be kind to God's kids, especially your brother Jesus.

December 10

QUIET TIME NOTES:

- God gives us enormously more than we give Him.
- "Realize who Jesus Christ is...Beware of refusing to go to the funeral of your own independence." —Oswald Chambers, *My Utmost for His Highest*
- "To him who overcomes I will give to eat from the tree of life...I will give him a white stone, and on the stone a new name written." —Revelation 2:7, 17 NKJV

My Takeaway:

God gives us enormously more than we give Him.

December 11

QUIET TIME NOTES:

- Self-love blocks God's love.
- Our individuality is a hard crust separating and isolating us from God.
- "How can we come to know God when our focus is elsewhere, on success, influence, and power?" —Henri J. Nouwen
- "Yet you have not returned to Me" appears five times in Amos 4. "Seek me and live" appears twice in Amos 5.
- "You have a reputation of being alive, but you are dead." —Revelation 3:1

My Takeaway:

Am I pretending to love God when I love myself more than I love Him?

December 12

QUIET TIME NOTES:

- Jesus enters hearts and heals battle scars.
- May we be content to share in the battle. God will examine our life for battle scars, not earthly success. —*Streams in the Desert*, my paraphrase
- "The days are coming," declares the Sovereign LORD, "when I will send a famine through the land…of hearing the words of the LORD." —Amos 8:11
- "See, I have placed before you an open door that no one can shut." —Revelation 3:8
- "Here I am! I stand at the door and knock. If anyone hears my voice and opens the door, I will come in…" —Revelation 3:20

My Takeaway:

Jesus enters hearts and heals battle scars. Open your door now.
Time is limited.

December 13

QUIET TIME NOTES:

- Truly trusting God transforms our life.
- "Someday we will know that the most exquisite work of our lives was done during those days when it was the darkest."
  —J.R. Miller, *Streams in the Desert*
- "God works for the good of those who love him."
  —Romans 8:28
- "God doesn't say all things are good. He says He can use all things for good for those who believe Him."
  —Lori Hatcher, *Crosswalk*
- "The pride of your heart has deceived you." —Obadiah 3

My Takeaway:

Truly trusting God transforms our life.

December 14

QUIET TIME NOTES:

- I can choose peace or problems. It depends on whom I depend upon.
- You can choose to replace oppressive, toxic thoughts with God's promises.
- "The Ninevites believed God." —Jonah 3:5
- "When God saw… how they turned from their evil ways, he relented." —Jonah 3:10
- "Forget the former things…I am making a way in the wilderness." —Isaiah 43:18-19
- "My peace I give you…Do not let your hearts be troubled." —John 14:27

My Takeaway:

I can choose peace or problems. It depends on whom I depend upon.

December 15

QUIET TIME NOTES:

- God trusts us and will help us.
- "Guard the good deposit that was entrusted to you—guard it with the help of the Holy Spirit who lives in us." —2 Timothy 1:14
- "God is our refuge and strength, an ever-present help in trouble. Therefore we will not fear…" —Psalm 46:1-2

My Takeaway:

God trusts us and will help us.

December 16

QUIET TIME NOTES:

- "A true Christian lives and labors not for himself, but for his neighbor." —Martin Luther
- "He has shown you, O man, what is good; and what does the LORD require of you but to do justly, to love mercy, and to walk humbly with your God?" —Micah 6:8 NKJV
- "The idols of the nations are silver and gold, the work of men's hands." —Psalm 135:15 NKJV
- "The Greatest Commandment requires our commitment as we make a contribution to the Great Commission." —Heard at Agape Outpost Church, Breckenridge, Colorado

My Takeaway:

The LORD requires us to serve those He loves, not what we love.

December 17

QUIET TIME NOTES:

- God gives if we ask.
- Most people think they're moral and spiritual and have no idea they're in desperate need of the gospel.
- On his deathbed Mickey Mantle was led to Christ by Bobby Richardson: "I am trusting in Christ's death to take me to heaven." He found life as he died—don't wait and miss life while you're alive.
- "Ask and it will be given to you." —Matthew 7:7
- "The old life is gone, a new life has begun!" —2 Corinthians 5:17 NLT
- "The one who calls you is faithful, and he will do it." —1 Thessalonians 5:24

My Takeaway:

God gives if we ask.

December 18

QUIET TIME NOTES:

- Only our obedience makes an eternal impact—everything else flies away.

- Doesn't it seem odd that we go to all this trouble to celebrate a birthday for someone we mostly ignore? —Girlfriends in God, my paraphrase

- "Do not wear yourself out to get rich…Cast but a glance at riches, and they are gone, for they will surely sprout wings and fly off…" —Proverbs 23:4

- We say God is in control, but we don't live like we believe it. It's not the work we do that counts; it's the obedience that counts.

- "Moses did all of those signs and wonders the LORD sent him to do." —Deuteronomy 34:11 (He obeyed!)

My Takeaway:

Give God a gift of obedience this year… and be blessed.

December 19

QUIET TIME NOTES:

- God will relent and rejoice when we repent.
- “I will…punish those who are complacent…Though they build houses, they will not live in them.” —Zephaniah 1:12-13
- “Before the decree takes effect…Seek the LORD…Seek righteousness, seek humility.” —Zephaniah 2:2-3
- “The Mighty One will save…He will rejoice over you with singing…[and] return your captives before your eyes.” —Zephaniah 3:17, 20 NKJV

My Takeaway:

God will relent and rejoice when we repent. (He can’t save us till we seek Him.)

December 20

QUIET TIME NOTES:

- Consider giving your heart to God this Christmas.
- This morning I asked God, "What is my part?" And He answered: "Give careful thought to your ways!" (Haggai 1:5.)
- "Search me, God, and know my heart…lead me."
—Psalm 139:23-24
- I ask myself, "Do I search my heart or just entertain myself?"
- People want blessings without the deep work of repentance and heart change.

My Takeaway:

Consider giving your heart to God this Christmas.

December 21

QUIET TIME NOTES:

- "You must let go of yesterday's mistakes in order to grasp today's blessings." —*The Word for You Today*
- "One thing I do: Forgetting what is behind and straining toward what is ahead…" —Philippians 3:13
- God saw Abraham "through a thick and dreadful darkness" (Genesis 15:12), and in the same way He sees us—through the night's darkened sky.
- Eagles are birds of solitude. God seeks "Eagle people"—who discover the mysteries of God through walking alone with Him. The Apostle John, after all, had to be banished to the island of Patmos to receive the Book of Revelation. Alone with God, our souls learn to soar. —My reflection after reading *Streams in the Desert*

My Takeaway:

Dark times can sparkle if we lift them up to God.

December 22

QUIET TIME NOTES:

- Trusting that God loves me unconditionally leads me to love others without conditions.
- Is there a list of conditions attached to my love?
- Putting confidence in myself will hinder me from trusting God.
- I will truly be able to love when I believe I am loved.
- “For you are all children of God through faith in Christ Jesus.” —Galatians 3:26 NLT

My Takeaway:

Trusting that God loves me unconditionally leads me to love to others without conditions.

December 23

QUIET TIME NOTES:

- Peace or panic: It all depends on the path I pick.
- You don't need all the answers to walk in peace. Get used to not knowing why!
- "You will go out in joy and be led forth in peace; the mountains and hills will burst into song before you." —Isaiah 55:12
- Disobedience always yields complications and confusion, panic instead of peace.
- "Trust in the Lord…he will make your paths straight." —Proverbs 3:5-6

My Takeaway:

Following God leads to peace; following myself leads to panic.

December 24

QUIET TIME NOTES:

- When I look past myself, I find God giving Himself.
- I view everything through the lens of eternity.
  HOPE = Having Our Perspective Eternal.
- What we experience doesn't always match the hope, but view it like a child: The morning's problems quickly give way to joy.
- You must get alone with God and decide if you want Him or yourself for Christmas.
- "Show me the way I should go, for to you I entrust my life."
  —Psalm 143:8
- The Peace of Christ has been gifted to you: Receive it.

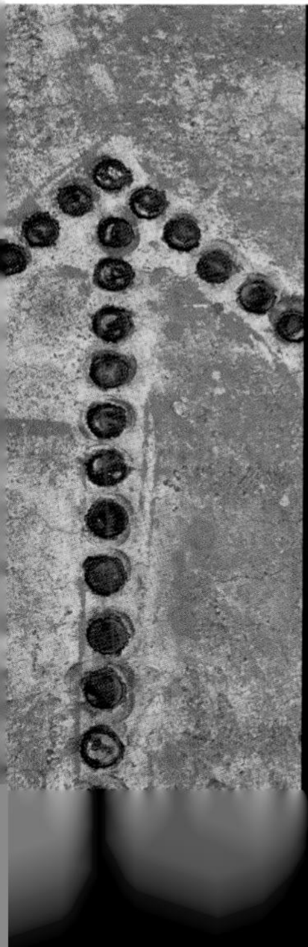

My Takeaway:

When I look past myself,
I find God giving Himself.
The greatest gift of
Christmas is wrapped in
quietness that allows God
to speak to your soul.

December 25

QUIET TIME NOTES:

As our kids were growing up, we moved 23 times, zigzagging across the country. It was interesting to see how each locale had a distinct style of Christmas decorating.

In the Midwest, folks used the big, old-fashioned multicolored bulbs. With snow in the background, it looked like a Currier and Ives Christmas print. Then we moved to Southern California, and we saw the most amazing thing! Folks hung long strands of lights from the tops of Coulter pines to the ground. Ingenious! Other states were all-white twinkle lights.

Later we moved to Dallas. All we had ever known about Christmas decorating looked painfully dull. Here every square inch is wrapped, glittered, and embellished, complete with soundtracks and moving reindeer. One house even had live reindeer.

One move from Philadelphia back to Dallas had us staying in a little rental house with one of the largest Live Oak trees I'd ever seen. Immediately, our 11-year-old son decided to have a decorating contest with our next-door neighbor. It took a solid week as he plastered the tree with every string of lights he could beg, borrow, and…no, he didn't steal, but you see where I'm going. Then the evening came to light up the houses for the first time. Both families assembled on the front lawn, we did the little drum roll, and then came the big moment.

It was glorious for a split second. Then in a flash, it was over—as the abundance of lights blew every fuse in the old house!

Later, I realized that *this glorious flash of light is what our life is like in the face of eternity*. What we do on earth will equal that millisecond flash of blazing light. Oh, that I always remember.

December 26

QUIET TIME NOTES:

- Hope is God's gift to us.
- I hope for renewal—from my self-centered, prayerless days, my wasted hours, and my slowness of heart.
- "The blood of Jesus, his Son, purifies us from all sin." —1 John 1:7 (Not only the sins I'm aware of, but deep, unconscious sin too.)
- There is no place we can hide our hearts from God, and when we are the most hopeless, He is the most strong.
- "There is one thing which gives radiance to everything. It is the idea of something around the corner." —G.K. Chesterton

My Takeaway:

The birth of Christ gives HOPE to each of us.

December 27

QUIET TIME NOTES:

- Sharing my messy life with God sets me free from it.
- The prison doors were broken down and all those bolted down were set free. (Acts 16:25-26.)
- "You, my brothers and sisters, were called to be free. But do not use your freedom to indulge the flesh; rather, serve one another humbly in love." —Galatians 5:13
- The God of creation condescends to talk with me, but He is never condescending.
- Even our worst days get better when we have a friend to share them with.

My Takeaway:

Confessing my messy life to God sets me free from it.

December 28

QUIET TIME NOTES:

- "There are only two types of men: the righteous who believe themselves sinners; the rest, sinners who believe themselves righteous." —Blaise Pascal
- Transformation is based on trusting, not trying. It's rooted in God's power, not willpower.
- "'Not by might nor by power, but by my Spirit,' says the LORD Almighty." —Zechariah 4:6
- A moment of truth marks you as either a disciple or a deserter.
- "From this time many of his disciples turned back and no longer followed him." —John 6:66
- "Books were opened…The dead were judged according to what they had done." —Revelation 20:12

My Takeaway:

God knows how we live and rewards accordingly. But thankfully, repentance brings freedom.

December 29

QUIET TIME NOTES:

- Our years show either commitment to God or contempt for God.

- As I cross the threshold of this next year, may I commit everything in my life—my soul, body, mind, friends, possessions—to God's loving care.

- "The LORD sustains the humble." —Psalm 147:6

- In this new year, even this day, may I welcome interruptions as invitations to serve.

- May I give the gift of myself to my friends.

My Takeaway:

Our years show either commitment to God or contempt for God.

December 30

QUIET TIME NOTES:

- "'Groans that words cannot express' (Romans 8:26) are often prayers God cannot refuse." —Charles H. Spurgeon
- "He will wipe every tear from their eyes." —Revelation 21:4
- "Have we not all one Father?...Why do we deal treacherously with one another?" —Malachi 2:10 NKJV
- "But the cowardly, the unbelieving, the vile, the murderers, the sexually immoral, those who practice magic arts, the idolaters and all liars—they will be consigned to the fiery lake of burning sulfur. This is the second death." —Revelation 21:8
- "Let us run with perseverance the race marked out for us." —Hebrews 12:1

My Takeaway:

God won't let the bad go unpunished or the good unrewarded. He will make all things right.

December 31

QUIET TIME NOTES:

- God gives a future of hope—and salvation. Praise Him!
- "Leave the broken, irreversible past in His hands, and step out into the invincible future with Him."
  —Oswald Chambers, *My Utmost for His Highest*
- "The LORD will go before you." —Isaiah 52:12
- "The…love of God our Savior appeared…so that…we might become heirs having the hope of eternal life." —Titus 3:4, 7
- "Call to me, and I will answer you, and show you great and mighty things, which you do not know." —Jeremiah 33:3 NKJV
- "Nevertheless, the time will come when I will heal Jerusalem's wounds and give it prosperity and peace." —Jeremiah 33:6 NLT

My Takeaway:

Don't relive your past. God gives a future of hope—and salvation.

With Immense Gratitude

What you hold in your hands is not the work of just me; it took God sitting with me at dawn as He guided and helped me to understand what He wanted to share with His child that day. I am in awe that His Holy Spirit would lead me on this treasure hunt each morning. My heart knows, and God knows, just how little of this comes out of my head! I am thankful for the generous and well-studied men and women from whose books and devotionals I have gained wisdom. Please see the complete list following these acknowledgements, as each is a remarkable guide to a richer spiritual life. I highly recommend each one, and I am in debt that they or their publishers each gave us permission to excerpt their work in *Jesus Confidential.*

I can assure you that this work would never be in your hands without my incredible editor, Julie Lyons. Her Spirit-filled life has taught me more than I care to admit. She is tenacious, highly skilled, and yet so kind in her encouragement of me and this work. *Jesus Confidential* could not have gone to print without her guidance and experience. The words "Thank you" are much too small.

Julie brought to our team two outstanding people. Jessica Johnson designed both the cover and the beautiful interior pages. I believe we will all be blessed by her work. And one of the hardest parts of preparing this book—tracking down all of the quotations and notes I used—was accomplished by editorial assistant Erin O'Day. I am grateful for her detailed work.

Finally, I'm so thankful for my friends who encouraged me early on to keep texting them to share what God had given me that day. Their heartfelt replies that these notes were exactly what they needed helped me to believe that God was pleased that I'd shared what He gave me.

As you can tell, this was a team effort, and I can assure you that I am the most blessed to have been part of this team.

With a grateful heart,

Sandy

Sources

All Scripture quotations, unless otherwise indicated, are taken from the Holy Bible, New International Version®, NIV®. Copyright ©1973, 1978, 1984, 2011 by Biblica, Inc.™ Used by permission of Zondervan. All rights reserved worldwide. www.zondervan.com. The "NIV" and "New International Version" are trademarks registered in the United States Patent and Trademark Office by Biblica, Inc.™

Scripture quotations marked NLT are taken from the Holy Bible, New Living Translation, copyright ©1996, 2004, 2015 by Tyndale House Foundation. Used by permission of Tyndale House Publishers, Carol Stream, Illinois 60188. All rights reserved.

Scripture quotations marked NKJV are taken from the Holy Bible, New King James Version®. Copyright ©1982 by Thomas Nelson. Used by permission. All rights reserved.

Several quotations were taken from the following pages of *Cowboy Ethics* by James P. Owen. Copyright © 2015 by James P. Owen. Used by permission of Skyhorse Publishing: p. 14, pp.40-41, pp. 44-45.

Several quotations were taken from posts by members of the Denison family. In order of appearance in *Jesus Confidential*, the quotes by Dr. Jim Denison (Dr. Jim Denison. © Denison Ministries. Source: denisonforum.org) were originally published on 1/31/19, 7/28/20, 12/3/20, 3/12/20, 5/4/20, 3/2/21, 3/26/21, 11/2/20, 11/25/20, 12/3/20; the quotes by Craig Denison (Craig Denison. © Denison Ministries. Source: first15.org) were originally published on 4/27/21, 9/18/20, 12/20/20; the quote by Janet Denison (Janet Denison. © Denison Ministries. Source: foundationswithjanet.org) was published on 11/11/20.

Excerpts from *Gates of Repentance: A New Union Prayerbook*, copyright © 1978, 1996 by the Central Conference of American Rabbis. Used by permission of the Central Conference of American Rabbis. All rights reserved.

Several quotations and paraphrases were taken from *God Calling* by A.J. Russell. Published by John Hunt Publishing Ltd. Reproduced with permission from John Hunt Publishing Ltd. In order of appearance by date in *Jesus Confidential*, followed by the corresponding page in *God Calling*: 6/16 (p. 246), 1/18 (p. 41), 6/22 (p. 253), 6/25 (p. 257), 4/24 (p. 171), 2/18 (p. 83), 6/10 (p. 236), 6/26 (p. 259), 7/28 (p. 300), 8/21 (p. 335), 8/22 (p. 336), 9/9 (p. 359), 9/27 (p. 380), 9/29 (p. 382), 10/28 (p. 418), 11/5 (p. 428), 11/27 (p. 454), 12/1 (p. 459), 12/2 (p. 460), 12/5 (p. 464).

Several quotations were taken from *Jesus Calling* by Sarah Young. Copyright © 2016 by Sarah Young. Used by permission of Thomas Nelson. www.thomasnelson.com.

Several quotations were taken from *Live in Grace, Walk in Love* by Bob Goff. Copyright © 2019 by Bob Goff. Used by permission of Thomas Nelson. www.thomasnelson.com.

Several quotations were taken from *My Utmost for His Highest*® by Oswald Chambers, edited by James Reimann, © 1992 by Oswald Chambers Publications Assn., Ltd., and used by permission of Our Daily Bread Publishing, Grand Rapids MI 49501. All rights reserved. The dates of the quotations in *My Utmost for His Highest*, in order of their appearance in *Jesus Confidential*, are as follows: 4/12, 4/14, 10/29, 6/10, 3/22, 3/20, 10/25, 9/28, 11/18, 11/23, 12/8, 12/9, 12/31.

Several quotations and/or paraphrases were taken from *Streams in the Desert* by L.B. Cowman, Copyright © 1997 by L.B. Cowman. Used by permission of Zondervan. www.zondervan.com. The page numbers of the quotations in *Streams in the Desert* are listed after their corresponding dates in *Jesus Confidential*: 1/4 (p. 18), 1/22 (p. 43), 7/3 (p. 260), 7/26 (p. 287), 8/13 (p. 309), 10/2 (p. 373), 10/8 (p. 381), 10/24 (p. 401), 10/29 (p. 407), 10/31 (p. 411), 11/16 (p. 429), 11/19 (p. 433), 11/21 (p. 436), 12/13 (p. 463).

Several quotations were taken from *Switch On Your Brain Every Day* by Dr. Caroline Leaf. Copyright © 2018 by Caroline Leaf. Used by permission of Baker Publishing Group, bakerpublishinggroup.com. The quotations were taken from the following dates: p. 245, Day 224; p. 36, Day 15; p. 45, Day 24; p. 47, Day 26; p. 51, Day 30; p. 28, Day 7; p. 67, Day 46; p. 128, Day 107; p. 154, Day 133; p. 225, Day 204; p. 228, Day 207.

Several quotations were taken from the following pages of *The Valley of Vision*, copyright Arthur Bennett, published by the Banner of Truth Trust, Edinburgh, UK. Banneroftruth.org: pp. 203, 205, 212, 214, 218, 79, 101, 9, 36, 51, 76, 107, 132, 106, 149, 160, 112, 167, 170.

Some quotations were taken from the following pages of *You are Blessed in the Names of God* by Sylvia Gunter. © 2018 by Sylvia Gunter. The Father's Business, P.O. Box 380333, Birmingham AL 35238, www.thefathersbusiness.com: pp. 7, 255.

Several quotations were taken from the following devotional dates of *The Father's Business Devotionals* by Sylvia Gunter. © 2020, 2021 by Sylvia Gunter. The Father's Business, P.O. Box 380333, Birmingham AL 35238, www.thefathersbusiness.com:12/16/20, 6/23/21, 11/9/20.

Several quotations were taken from *You Are the Beloved: Daily Meditations for Spiritual Living* by Henri J.M. Nouwen, compiled and edited by Gabrielle Earnshaw, copyright © 2017 by The Henri Nouwen Legacy Trust. Used by permission of Convergent Books, an imprint of Random House, a division of Penguin Random House LLC. All rights reserved. In order of their appearance in *Jesus Confidential*, followed by the page numbers in *You Are the Beloved*: 1/22 (p. 24), 11/15 (p. 349), 11/18 (p. 352), 12/11 (p. 377).

The following quotations and paraphrases were taken from The Word for You Today. They are listed in order of their appearance in *Jesus Confidential*:

"Sometimes your greatest blessings come from your most negative circumstances...Let your emotions subside—before you decide."
Taken from THE WORD FOR YOU TODAY—Bob Gass Copyright (c) Celebration Enterprises, June 13, 2020. Used by permission of The Word For You Today, www.wordforyou.com

God gives seed to sowers, not hoarders (paraphrase).
Taken from THE WORD FOR YOU TODAY—Bob Gass Copyright (c) Celebration Enterprises, June 19, 2020. Used by permission of The Word For You Today, www.wordforyou.com

"The opposite of courage isn't fear, it's conformity."
Taken from THE WORD FOR YOU TODAY—Bob Gass Copyright (c) Celebration Enterprises, June 27, 2021. Used by permission of The Word For You Today, www.wordforyou.com

"Chances are, if you're feeling disheartened, it's because you are thinking gloomy thoughts. If you want to feel uplifted, make a concerted effort to think uplifting thoughts."
Taken from THE WORD FOR YOU TODAY—Bob Gass Copyright (c) Celebration Enterprises, December 12, 2020. Used by permission of The Word For You Today, www.wordforyou.com

"Depression, gloom, pessimism, despair, and discouragement stop more people than all the world's combined illnesses...you can never be defeated unless you're defeated in your thinking."
Taken from THE WORD FOR YOU TODAY—Bob Gass Copyright (c) Celebration Enterprises, December 13, 2020. Used by permission of The Word For You Today, www.wordforyou.com

"People who spend their lives 'waiting for their ship to come in' are usually disappointed—or die on the pier."
Taken from THE WORD FOR YOU TODAY—Bob Gass Copyright (c) Celebration Enterprises, December 15, 2020. Used by permission of The Word For You Today, www.wordforyou.com

"The only way to keep what you have is to give it away."
Taken from THE WORD FOR YOU TODAY—Bob Gass Copyright (c) Celebration Enterprises, December 21, 2020. Used by permission of The Word For You Today, www.wordforyou.com

"You can't love in a hurry."
Taken from THE WORD FOR YOU TODAY by Keri Wyatt Kent—Bob Gass Copyright (c) Celebration Enterprises, December 29, 2020. Used by permission of The Word For You Today, www.wordforyou.com

"A race toward the finish line has a different sense of purpose and urgency than a jog around the block."
Taken from THE WORD FOR YOU TODAY by Carolyn Arends—Bob Gass Copyright (c) Celebration Enterprises, March 25, 2021. Used by permission of The Word For You Today, www.wordforyou.com

"Sometimes we are in such a hurry to 'fix' people we don't have time to sympathize with them."
Taken from THE WORD FOR YOU TODAY—Bob Gass Copyright (c) Celebration Enterprises, February 9, 2021. Used by permission of The Word For You Today, www.wordforyou.com

"Most of our worries can be summed up in two words: 'What if?'"
Taken from THE WORD FOR YOU TODAY—Bob Gass Copyright (c) Celebration Enterprises, June 30, 2021. Used by permission of The Word For You Today, www.wordforyou.com

Don't give your leftovers to God—give your first fruits. Leftovers are tied to self-sufficiency while first-fruit giving is God's sufficiency (paraphrase).
Taken from THE WORD FOR YOU TODAY—Bob Gass Copyright (c) Celebration Enterprises, January 25, 2021. Used by permission of The Word For You Today, www.wordforyou.com

"We don't like to wait for anything, including God...While we are waiting, God is working. The sign on God's waiting room reads, 'Be still, and know that I am God (Psalm 46:10).'"
Taken from THE WORD FOR YOU TODAY—Bob Gass Copyright (c) Celebration Enterprises, August 8, 2021. Used by permission of The Word For You Today, www.wordforyou.com

You won't find the words I, me, my, or mine in the Lord's Prayer. But you do find "give us," "forgive us," and "deliver us." God knows what you want and why you want it (paraphrase).
Taken from THE WORD FOR YOU TODAY—Bob Gass Copyright (c) Celebration Enterprises, February 4, 2021. Used by permission of The Word For You Today,www.wordforyou.com

"You can't pray, 'Lord, what do you want to do?' when you already know what to do but aren't willing to do it, but won't do it. If you're serious about getting your prayers answered, read the fine print!"
Taken from THE WORD FOR YOU TODAY—Bob Gass Copyright (c) Celebration Enterprises, February 5, 2021. Used by permission of The Word For You Today, www.wordforyou.com

"Unconfessed, unforgiven sin will make you miserable."
Taken from THE WORD FOR YOU TODAY—Bob Gass Copyright (c) Celebration Enterprises, February 13, 2020. Used by permission of The Word For You Today, www.wordforyou.com

"Prize fighter James Corbett was once asked, 'What's the most important thing for a man to do to become a champion?' He replied, 'Fight one more round.'"
Taken from THE WORD FOR YOU TODAY—Bob Gass Copyright (c) Celebration Enterprises, February 16, 2021. Used by permission of The Word For You Today, www.wordforyou.com

"The same wind that blew at your back on your way to hell will blow in your face on your way to heaven."
Taken from THE WORD FOR YOU TODAY—Bob Gass Copyright (c) Celebration Enterprises, February 17, 2021. Used by permission of The Word For You Today, www.wordforyou.com

"God expects nothing from you but failure!...But He has given the Holy Spirit to you so that you need not fail."
Taken from THE WORD FOR YOU TODAY—Bob Gass Copyright (c) Celebration Enterprises [February 19, 2021]. Used by permission of The Word For You Today, www.wordforyou.com

"Outrunning your rival doesn't mean you ran your best race."
Taken from THE WORD FOR YOU TODAY—Bob Gass Copyright (c) Celebration Enterprises, July 6, 2021. Used by permission of The Word For You Today, www.wordforyou.com

"Hell begins on the day God grants us a clear vision of all we might have achieved...the gifts we wasted...and all we might have done but didn't do."
Taken from THE WORD FOR YOU TODAY—Bob Gass Copyright (c) Celebration Enterprises, February 22, 2021. Used by permission of The Word For You Today, www.wordforyou.com

"If you're on the wrong train, don't keep going—get off at the next station!"
Taken from THE WORD FOR YOU TODAY—Bob Gass Copyright (c) Celebration Enterprises, February 23, 2021. Used by permission of The Word For You Today, www.wordforyou.com

"One half of knowing what you want is knowing what you must give up before you get it."
—American playwright Sidney Howard
Taken from THE WORD FOR YOU TODAY—Bob Gass Copyright (c) Celebration Enterprises, February 28, 2021. Used by permission of The Word For You Today, www.wordforyou.com

"God dispenses His goodness not with an eyedropper but with a fire hydrant."
Taken from THE WORD FOR YOU TODAY—Bob Gass Copyright (c) Celebration Enterprises, March 4, 2021. Used by permission of The Word For You Today, www.wordforyou.com

"You must let go of yesterday's mistakes in order to grasp today's blessings."
Taken from THE WORD FOR YOU TODAY—Bob Gass Copyright (c) Celebration Enterprises, March 21, 2021. Used by permission of The Word For You Today, www.wordforyou.com